Francis Turner Palgrave

The Visions of England

Francis Turner Palgrave

The Visions of England

ISBN/EAN: 9783744712408

Printed in Europe, USA, Canada, Australia, Japan

Cover: Foto ©ninafisch / pixelio.de

More available books at **www.hansebooks.com**

THE
VISIONS
OF
ENGLAND

BY

FRANCIS T. PALGRAVE

*LATE FELLOW OF EXETER COLLEGE
OXFORD*

—TANTA RES EST, UT PAENE
VITIO MENTIS TANTUM OPUS
INGRESSUS MIHI VIDEAR.

London
MACMILLAN AND CO.
1881

TO THE NAMES OF

HENRY HALLAM AND FRANCIS PALGRAVE

FRIENDS AND FELLOW-LABOURERS IN ENGLISH HISTORY

FOR FORTY YEARS,

WHO, DIFFERING OFTEN IN JUDGMENT,

WERE AT ONE THROUGHOUT LIFE IN DEVOTED LOVE OF

JUSTICE, TRUTH, AND ENGLAND,

IN AFFECTIONATE AND REVERENT REMEMBRANCE

THIS BOOK IS INSCRIBED AND DEDICATED

PREFACE

As the scheme which the Author has here endeavoured to execute has not, so far as he knows, the advantage of any direct precedent in any literature, he hopes that a few explanatory words may be offered without incurring censure for egotism.

Our history is so eminently rich and varied, and at the same time, by the fact of our insular position, so stamped with unity, that from days very remote it has supplied matter for song. To judge by the still surviving fragments, single events, which moved men of English or Celtic blood deeply, were the earliest subjects thus dealt with; and the true instincts of spontaneous art guided the poets to a lyrical treatment. The Norman conquest of England, and the English conquest of Wales, slackened or broke up these primitive efforts; and when we reach the gradual settlement of the island into the forms which it has since substantially retained, awakening national self-consciousness, we find, was followed by a series of endeavours to render our history in consecutive annalistic verse. We have very few lyrics, even if we here include the ballad in its genuine form, and those rarely of value, upon single incidents or heroes, during the long period between that Layamon of

Earnley, who near seven centuries since, devoted himself to 'tell the noble deeds of England' in chronicle fashion, and those many eminent writers who, when once more the nation's consciousness of itself was vividly roused in the Elizabethan age, again, under Renaissance influences, attempted to set the *Gesta Anglorum* to the music of poetical narrative. Whilst recognizing the genius and ability often shown in this immense field between the third Henry and the first James, it must, on the whole, be confessed that in no instance was the aim attained. Those 'two by-ways,' as Schiller has termed them, 'the prosaical and the rhetorical,' were not and could not be sufficiently avoided. Hence no national epic, no poem which, as a whole, really touched the country, has been left us. It is in the plays of Shakespeare only that we find living pictures of our magnificent early history; whilst it has been reserved for a great contemporary by the prerogative of genius to remodel and to vivify in splendid verse the mythical glory and gloom of the Arthurian Epos.

Failure was, indeed, inevitable in the attempt to put a history into verse, for the reasons which proved fatal to the Roman *Annals* of Ennius, (a poet probably more powerful than any of our own metrical chroniclers), and which, we may conjecture, deterred Vergil from the similar task pressed upon him by Augustus. A nation's history cannot but present many dull or confused periods, many men and things intractable by poetry, though, perhaps, politically effective and important, which cannot, however, be excluded from any narrative aiming at consecutiveness; and, by the natural laws of art, these passages, when rendered in verse, in their effect become more prosaic than they would be in a prose rendering. And to the general recognition of these difficulties we may reasonably ascribe the gradual cessation of historical poetry on the annalistic or didactic model during the last two hundred years :—although, meanwhile, our history,—the true Epic of England,—studied with more than former ability and devotion, has been unrolled before us in its splendours and its shadows with a force and a truth heretofore unattained, and with the promise of yet greater completeness.

Reviewing, then, this experience of centuries, and feeling deeply that the material before an Englishman, in its insular unity, variety, and wealth, is a field greatly wider and more fruitful than even that which lay before a Homer or a Herodotus, a Livy or a Vergil, a new departure, I have thought, might be essayed. My attempt has therefore been to revert to the earlier and more natural conditions of poetry, and to offer,—not a continuous narrative; not poems on every critical moment or conspicuous man in our long annals,—but single lyrical pictures of such leading or typical characters and scenes in English history, and only such, as have seemed to me amenable to a strictly poetical treatment. Poetry, not History, has, hence, been my first and last aim; or, perhaps I might define it, History for Poetry's sake. At the same time, I have striven to keep throughout as closely to absolute historical truth in the design and colouring of the pieces as the exigencies of poetry permit. To grasp this double end, my endeavour, by a wide and careful course of reading, and aided by what local or other knowledge I could bring into use, has been to enter, in each case, within the atmosphere of the age,—to penetrate and be penetrated by, the passion of the moment:

—and then, finding, if possible, the right motive and (if the phrase be allowed) the right angle of presentation, with the metrical form most congenial to the subject,—to set forth each scene or character in its essential truth :—uniting at once the actual tone and spirit of the time concerned, with the best estimate which has been reached by the research and genius of modern investigators.

This aim has governed and limited both the selection and the treatment of my subjects. The choice has necessarily fallen, almost wholly, not on picturesque incident or unfamiliar character, but on the men and things that we think of first, when thinking of our 'island story,'—or upon such as represent and symbolize the main current of it. Themes, however, on which able or popular song is already extant,—notably in case of Scotland,—I have in general avoided. In the rendering, my strenuous desire has been always to rest the poetry of each Vision on its own intrinsic interest ; to write, as I must think the great writers of the great ages have ever written,—at any rate upon matter of this nature,—with a straightforward eye to the object alone; not studious of ornament for ornament's sake; allowing the least possible overt intrusion of the writer's personality; 'preferring,' in the old phrase, 'the Muses to the Sirens;' and convinced that the truest pathos lies in the situation, not in the pathetic setting forth,—the truest poetry, not in the decorative overlay, but in the form and matter ;—that, in a word, for the subject before me, it is in the truth of history that the romance of history is to be discovered.

In accordance with lyrical law, I have, as a rule, sought to fix upon some definite motive, some actual picture, for each piece,—something, in short, which naturally suggests a poem without any thought of series,—and to unite this with contiguous events and persons, and with the general colour of the period, by a free use of that allusive element which, at all times, has been one of the special prerogatives of the Lyric. So much,—I fear, too much,—of pure historical allusion has hence entered into the work, that I have almost wholly neglected the resource, easier to the writer than to the reader, of archaeological phrase or reference:—and this the more willingly, because details of architecture or dress, of professions and customs, though materials indispensable for historical art, yet, if allowed prominence in the picture, are apt to conceal that essential identity of man with man throughout all known ages which underlies poetry not less than history. And, as an antiquarian device, I have also avoided attempting that dramatic reproduction of the past in its actual literary forms and language, which has given us a few masterpieces, (yet not, I venture to think, wholly satisfactory or free from a suspicion of unreality and artifice), at the hands of Scott and of Macaulay.

It is common to the Fine Arts, that the more large or enlargeable are their technical powers, the more rigidly must the artist restrain himself in the use of them; the silent sense of difficulty conquered, of perfect freedom within the strictest limits,—of Liberty identified with Necessity,— (if I may be permitted a phrase which goes to the root of the matter),—being one great element in that pleasure which, however variously we may define it, is yet the eternal aim of art. Hence, perhaps, the comparatively small number of stanza-systems which seem to have been ordinarily employed by the Greeks, to whose exquisite quantitative language endless forms would have been possible. Our poetry, dependent for its rhythm, not on fixed syllabic quantity, but on accent, by terminal rhyme has to supply an equivalent for the quantitative structure of classical verse: this element in modern language being so vague and fluent, that, comparing the effect of the Greek or Latin poetry, a *general impression* that our metre is iambic,—anapaestic and dactylic, —or trochaic (◡́: ◡◡́, ◌́◡◡: ◌́◡) will be found almost all that we can effectually maintain. The innumerable rhymed lyrical systems which it is the pride of English poetry to possess are, hence, a lawful compensation for our poverty in the ancient, ever-varied, rhythmical sequence of sounds within the body of the verse itself. We satisfy the requirement of 'Liberty with Necessity,' in the field of metre, far more by terminal than by structural contrivance and arrangement.

Of this metrical wealth, in a series so varied in appeal as the following, I have endeavoured to avail myself;—there being, doubtless, could we find it, some one system which will most naturally clothe every subject,—be its authentic outward voice. 'Purity,' that is, strictness, 'of metre,' said the great German Thinker and Poet whom I have before quoted, ' serves as a sensuous representation of the inner necessity ' —(by which Schiller intends the essential poetry)—' of the ' thought.' Despite some splendid exceptions, from the *Danae* of Simonides, (at any rate, as that marvellous fragment has survived),—to Dryden's *Feast*, Wordsworth's *Immortality*, or Tennyson's *Wellington*, the irregular, arrhythmical lyric seems to me ever to want this essential purity, this severity, of metre: whilst, when the language is accentual, not quantitative, in character, the unrhymed irregular lyric, with its even more unsatisfactory sister, the bastard modern hexameter,—whatever the value of the contents,—appear to me forms which barely merit the great name of Poetry. The great facility of execution, (essentially antagonistic to the sense of *inner necessity*), permitted by their lax structure is, in fact, what in recent days has recommended these metrical systems,—together with the narrative (as distinct from the lyrical) ballad, which,—charming as the genuine expression of an early age,—like certain wild flowers, is almost always denaturalized by culture. Whilst, however, excluding all these indolences of metre, I have also excluded those highly-complex schemes of lyric which we owe to Dorian artists; and, with them, the beautiful modified varieties mostly due to the exquisite genius of Gray. Stanzas so elaborate require, in truth, the choral accessories, the music and the dance to explain them to ear and eye,—in view of which Arion, Pindar, or Stesichorus wrote,—if they are to be pleasurably comprehensible. As therefore Horace, even in his impersonal lyrics, went back to the simpler Aeolic models which preceded the choral ode, so here resort has been made, in general, to native forms of stanza:—although where the subject seemed of itself imperatively to require some peculiar, perhaps novel, arrangement in metre and rhyme, or even the (symmetrical) use of more than one system, I have ventured upon essays which are commended to the reader's kindly judgment.

By those who hold with the writer that strict conformity to its own technical rules and material necessities is the primary canon in every Fine Art, these remarks will have been already excused. Turning now from treatment to subject-matter once more, from the vehicle to the contents, —whilst I could not, without folly, make any claim to the position and authority of the historical scholar;—whilst Poetry, not History, has been my object;—yet my earnest effort everywhere and always has been in no instance to sacrifice History to the higher Muse, or to set forth any aspect deviating from the best decision which in each case I could attain. Truth, in fact, might be described as the moral end of Poetry herself: Truth, if rendered and embodied by her imaginative insight, being confessedly and by natural right more vital,—purer, deeper, and wider,—than what human power by any other method can grasp or render. Truth, therefore,—History exorcised from the demon of party-spirit,—I have been doubly bound to do my best to reach. And I would hence beg a certain forbearance, if anywhere these Visions do not correspond with the results of a reader's own historical research. Especially I ask this where the Seventeenth Century is concerned. Here, after careful and (I hope) unbiassed study, in regard to some leading points rather of character and motive than of fact, I have ventured to dissent from opinions current during the last fifty years, and to return, in the main, to the views set forth by that deep and high-souled thinker whose friendship I also, with my Father, shared the privilege of enjoying.—But a criticism upon this vast and difficult subject, (even were it within my power), would be here out of place:—for some further suggestions I refer the reader to the *Appendix*, and will here add only the conviction that the research which Mr. S. Rawson Gardiner is now gradually giving, for the first time, to this section of our history in its full sense,—for the constitutional side alone was dealt with by Hallam,—will tend to confirm the honour in which I have held that historian. We have had narrators more dramatically brilliant; evidence is before us which was not before Mr. Hallam; traditional feeling may have, here and there, led him astray;—yet he still remains the one man of even weight and balance; singly and eminently, *justissimus unus.*

To define the scope of what this series attempts, is, in itself, a confession of presumptuousness,—the writer's own sense of which is but feebly and imperfectly expressed in the words from Vergil's letter to Augustus prefixed as my motto. In truth, so rich and so wide are the materials, that to scheme a lyrical series which should really paint the *Gesta Anglorum* in their fullness might almost argue 'lack of wit,' *vitium mentis,* in much greater powers than mine. So far, however, as the essay has been here adventured, I shall at least hope that the love of truth and the love of England are mine by inheritance in a degree sufficient to exempt this book, (the labour of several years), from infidelity to either :—that, whatever the defects of execution, the intrinsic worth and weight of the subject may, in its measure, commend these songs, both at home, and in the many Englands beyond sea, to some, perhaps, among those who, despite the inevitably more engrossing attractions of the Present, and the emphatic bias of modern culture towards the immediate and the tangible, maintain that high and soul-inspiring interest which identifies us with our magnificent Past :—that, finally, I have been faithful to that noblest function of Poetry, when she does justice to long-slighted merit, or humbles undeserved pride; shames the oppressor and his eulogists, and gives the crown to the forgotten victim;—purifying the mind 'by pity and 'by terror':—taking as my device the words of that great predecessor who did for the legends of Hellas what it has been my endeavour to do for the history of my own country ;

———Χρυσὸν εὔχονται, πεδίον δ' ἕτεροι
ἀπέραντον· ἐγὼ δ' ἀστοῖς ἀδὼν καὶ χθονὶ γυῖα καλύψαιμ',
αἰνέων αἰνητά, μομφὰν δ' ἐπισπείρων ἀλιτροῖς.

F. T. P.

12 Sep. 1881
LITTLE PARK
LYME REGIS

CONTENTS

	PAGE
PRELUDE	1
THE FIRST AND LAST LAND	8
THE DREAM OF MAXEN WLEDIG	10
GARIANONUM	20
PAULINUS AND EDWIN	26
ALFRED THE GREAT	29
A DANISH BARROW	32
HASTINGS	34
DEATH IN THE FOREST	42
EDITH OF ENGLAND	46
LE CHATEAU GAILLARD	49
A CRUSADER'S TOMB	53
A BALLAD OF EVESHAM	57
THE DIRGE OF LLYWELYN	60
THE REJOICING OF THE LAND	63

CONTENTS

	PAGE
CRECY	74
THE BLACK DEATH	77
THE PILGRIM AND THE PLOUGHMAN	82
JEANNE D'ARC	90
TOWTON FIELD	93
GROCYN AT OXFORD	96
MARGARET TUDOR	104
LONDON BRIDGE	107
A BALLAD OF QUEEN CATHARINE	113
AT FOUNTAINS	116
SIR HUGH WILLOUGHBY	119
LADY CATHERINE'S LAMENT	124
CROSSING SOLWAY	127
SIDNEY AT ZUTPHEN	133
ELIZABETH AT TILBURY	139
EL DORADO	142
PRINCE CHARLES AT THE LOUVRE	154
AT BEMERTON	157
PRINCESS ANNE	160
AFTER CHALGROVE FIGHT	167
A CHURCHYARD IN OXFORDSHIRE	171
MARSTON MOOR	179

CONTENTS

	PAGE
THE FUGITIVE KING	182
THE CAPTIVE CHILD	185
THE MOURNING MUSES	189
THE WRECK OF THE ADMIRAL	193
DUNNOTTAR CASTLE	196
THE RETURN OF LAW	199
THE POET'S EUTHANASIA	215
WHITEHALL GALLERY	217
THE BALLAD OF KING MONMOUTH	220
WILLELMUS VAN NASSAU	224
A DIRGE OF REPENTANCE	227
THE CHILDLESS MOTHER	233
BLENHEIM	237
AT HURSLEY IN MARDEN	243
THE TOWER OF DOOM	247
WOLFE AT QUEBEC	250
JOHNSON AND THOSE ABOUT HIM	254
CHARLES EDWARD AT ROME	259
SIMPLICITY	267
TRAFALGAR	271
THE DEATH OF SIR JOHN MOORE	277
TORRES VEDRAS	281

	PAGE
ART AND NATURE	286
THE VALLEY OF DEATH	289
THE SOLDIERS' BATTLE	295
AFTER CAWNPORE	300
MOUNT VERNON	305
SANDRINGHAM	310
A DORSET IDYL	314
THINGS VISIBLE AND INVISIBLE	320
A SUMMER SUNSET	327
A HOME IN THE PALACE	329
ENGLAND ONCE MORE	335
APPENDIX	339

THE VISIONS OF ENGLAND

PRELUDE:

Caesar to Egbert

ENGLAND, fair England! Empress isle of isles!
—Round whom the loving-envious ocean plays,
Girdling thy feet with silver and with smiles,
Whilst all the nations crowd thy liberal bays;
On rushing wheel and heart of flame they come,
Or glide and glance like white-wing'd doves that know
    And seek their proper home:—
England! not England yet! but fair as now,
When first the chalky strand was stirr'd by Roman prow.

On thy dear countenance, great mother-land,
Age after age thy sons have set their sign,
Moulding the features with successive hand
Not always sedulous of beauty's line:—
And yet Man's art in one harmonious aim
With Nature's gentle moulding, here has work'd
    A perfect whole to frame:

Nor does earth's labour'd face elsewhere, like thee,
Give back her children's heart with such full sympathy.

On marshland rough and self-sprung forest gazed
The imperial Roman of the eagle eye;
Log-splinter'd forts on green hill-summits raised,
Earth huts and rings that dot the chalk-downs high :—
Dark rites of hidden faith in grove and moor;
Idols of monstrous frame; rude carts of war;
    Rock tombs and pillars hoar :
Strange races, Finn, Iberian, Belgae, Celt;
While in the wolds huge bulls and antler'd giants dwelt.

Another age !—The spell of Rome has past
Transforming all our Britain; Ruthless plough,
Which plough'd the world, yet o'er the nations cast
The seed of arts, and law, and all that now
Has ripen'd into commonwealths :—Her hand
With network mile-paths binding plain and hill
    Arterialized the land :
The thicket yields; the soil for use is clear;
Peace with her plastic touch,—field, farm, and grange
    are here.

Lo, flintwall'd cities, castles stark and square
Bastion'd with rocks that rival Nature's own;

Red-furnaced baths, trim gardens planted fair
With tree and flower the North ne'er yet had known;
Long temple-roofs with statues wing'd on high
Like pinnacles of living gold that seem
      To shake in summer sky :—
The land had rest, while conquering legions lay
By northern ramparts camp'd, and held the Pict at bay.

Imperious Empire! Thrice-majestic Rome!
No later age, as earth's slow centuries glide,
Can raze the footprints stamp'd where thou hast come,
The ne'er repeated grandeur of thy stride!
—Though now so dense a darkness takes the land,
Law, peace, wealth, letters, faith,—all lights are quench'd
      By violent heathen hand :—
Vague warrior kings; names writ in fire and wrong;
Aurelius, Urien, Ida;—shades of ancient song.

And Thou—O whether born of flame and wave,
Or Gorlois' son, or Uther's, blameless lord,
True knight, who died for those thou couldst not save
When the Round Table brake their plighted word,—
The lord of song has set thee in thy grace
And glory, rescued from the phantom world,
      Before us face to face;

No more Avilion bowers the King detain;
The mystic child returns; the Arthur reigns again!

—Now, as some cloud that hides a mountain bulk
Thins to white smoke, and mounts in lighten'd air,
And through the veil the gray enormous hulk
Burns, and the summit last is keen and bare,—
From wasted Britain so the gloaming clears;
Another birth of time breaks eager out,
    And England fair appears:—
Imperial youth great on her golden brow,
While the prophetic eyes with hope and promise glow.

Then from the wild waste places of the land,
Charr'd skeletons of cities, shatter'd walls
Of Roman strength, and towers that darkly stand
Of that lost world survivors, forth she calls
Her new creation:—O'er the land is wrought
The happy villagedom by English tribes
    From Elbe and Baltic brought;
Red kine light up to life the ravaged plain;
The forest glooms are pierced; the plough-land laughs
    again.

Each from its little croft the homesteads peep,
Green apple-garths around, and hedgeless meads,

Smooth-shaven lawns of ever-shifting sheep,
Wolds where his dappled crew the swineherd feeds :—
Pale gold round pure pale foreheads, and their eyes
More dewy blue than speedwell by the brook
    When Spring's fresh current flies,
The free fair maids come barefoot to the fount,
Or poppy-crown'd with fire, the car of harvest mount.

On the salt stream that rings us, ness and bay,
The nation's old sea-soul beats blithe and strong;
The black foam-breasters taste Biscayan spray,
And where 'neath Polar dawns the narwhals throng :—
Free hands, free hearts, for labour and for glee,
Or village-moot, when thane with churl unites
    Beneath the sacred tree;
While wisdom tempers force, and bravery leads,
Till spears beat *Aye!* on shields, and words at once are deeds.

Again with life the ruin'd cities smile,
Again from mother-Rome their sacred fire
Knowledge and Faith rekindle through the isle,
Nigh quench'd by barbarous war and heathen ire :—
—No more on Balder's grave let Anglia weep
When winter storms entomb the golden year
    Sunk in Adonis-sleep;

Another God has risen, and not in vain!
The Woden-ash is low: the Cross asserts her reign.

—Land of the most law-loving,—the most free!
My dear, dear England! sweet and green as now,
The flower-illumined garden of the sea,
And Nature least impair'd by axe and plough!
A laughing land!—Thou seest not in the north
How the black Dane and vulture Norseman wait
    The sign of coming forth,
The foul Landeyda flap its raven plume,
And all the realms once more eclipsed in pagan gloom!

—O race, of many races well compact!
As some rich stream that runs in silver down
From the White Mount:—his baby steps untrack'd
Where clouds and azure cliffs of crystal frown;
Now, alien founts bring tributary flood,
Or kindred waters blend their native hue,
    Some darkening as with blood;
These fraught with iron strength and freshening brine,
And these with sweeter waves, to purify and refine.

Now calm as strong, and clear as summer air,
Blessing and blest of earth and sky, he glides:
Now on some rock-ridge rends his bosom fair,
And foams with cloudy wrath and hissing tides:

Then gathering up his beauty and his force
The bitter sweetness of life's music bears
  Down the long seaward course :—
So through Time's mead, great River, greatly glide :
Whither, thou may'st not know :—but He, who knows, will guide.

Northern ramparts: That of Agricola and Lollius Urbicus from Forth to Clyde, and the greater work of Hadrian and Severus between Tyne and Solway.

The happy villagedom: See the animated description in Green's *History of the English People*, B. I : ch. i.

Village-moot: Held on a little hill or round a sacred tree : ' the ' ealdermen spoke, groups of freemen stood round, clashing shields ' in applause, settling matters by loud shouts of *Aye* or *Nay ;* ' (*Green :* B. I : ch. i).

No more on Balder's grave: See Kemble's *Saxons in England*, B. I : ch. xii.

The foul Landeyda: Name of Danish banner : ' the desolation ' of the land.'

THE FIRST AND LAST LAND

THRICE-BLEST, alone with Nature!—here, where gray
    Belerium fronts the spray
Smiting the bastion'd crags through centuries flown,
    While, 'neath the hissing surge,
Ocean sends up a deep, deep undertone,

As though his heavy chariot-wheels went round:
    Nor is there other sound
Save from the abyss of air, a plaintive note,
    The seabirds' calling cry,
As down the wind with well-poised weight they float,

Or on some white-fringed reef set up their post,
    And sentinel the coast:—
Whilst, round each jutting cape, in pillar'd file,
    The lichen-bearded rocks
Like hoary giants guard the sacred Isle.

—Happy, alone with Nature, thus!—Yet here
    Dim, primal man is near;—
The hawk-eyed eager traders, who of yore
    Through long Biscayan waves
Steer'd cautious from the Gaditanian shore

Or the Sidonian, with their fragrant freight
    Oil-olive, fig, and date;
Jars of dark sunburnt wine, flax-woven robes,
    Or Tyrian azure glass
Wavy with gold, and agate-banded globes :—

Changing for amber-knobs their Eastern ware
    Or tin-sand silvery fair,
To temper brazen swords, or rim the shield
    Of heroes, arm'd for fight :—
While the rough miners, wondering, gladly yield

The treasured ore; nor Alexander's name
    Know, nor fair Helen's shame;
Or in his tent how Peleus' wrathful son
    Looks toward the sea, nor heeds
The towers of still-unconquer'd Ilion.

Belerium: The name given to the Land's End by Diodorus. He describes the natives as hospitable and civilized. They mined tin, which was bought by traders and carried through Gaul to the south-east. But the sceptical mind of Sir G. C. Lewis was not satisfied that the Phoenicians themselves reached England :—(*Astronomy of the Ancients:* pp. 452, 3, 5).

THE DREAM OF MAXEN WLEDIG

383

Lord of the Seven Hills, and the ruddy river below,
Lord of the whole round world, and the streams that over it go,
Maximus rides to the chase, and thirty kings at his side,
Thirty and more, proud vassals of Rome, by the Emperor ride:
And the hunt up the valley rings, the coverts of deer and of boar,
Blaring of horns, and shouts, and Molossian musical roar.
But the strong sun enter'd his brain; 'neath a briar he laid him, and slept:
On the lances they hung their shields, and the guardian palisade kept,
Fending him so, and hushing the hounds: and he dream'd, as he lay.

Him thought, by the stream that narrow'd along its rough narrowing way
Still upward he clomb, till it wanes to a thread, and the snow-blink around
Sends up its false day to the sky, and the snow-quakes in thunder resound,

And rocks lean out, and firs on the rocks; till the tree-
world is left,
And life to the wind-grass retreats, and the crimson-cup
moss in the cleft;
And a myriad boulders are strown at his feet from the
dreary moraine,
As spirits set fast in granite and silence of motionless pain :
And solitude hums and presses around, and he feels as
if two,
Himself and his soul there beside, were alone with the
rocks and the blue :
And the giants are frowning above, and silver spires arise
Like palace-fountains of spray; and his path goes up to
the skies.
And now from the topmost top o'er forest and plain he
looks forth,
Tilth and pasture and rivers that coil and flash to the
north :—
And he journey'd and came to the mouth of the widest,
the bridgeless and free,
And the City of Towers, between the two horns it push'd
to the sea;
And a Castle of rainbow colours o'er all tower'd into the
sky,
And a ship like a swan lay tossing and chafing and straining to fly;

And the fairest island of islands before him across the
 blue neck
Rose like a silver wall, and Maxen leapt on the deck;
And as a dream in a dream the galley ran o'er the foam,
And his feet on the island were light with delight; and
 he knew it was Home.

Then again he tracks a great stream from the mouth to
 the fountain; again
Treads o'er the clouds, the high peak of the eagles, and
 looks on the main:
Sees a fair castle beneath, a crown of towers that run
Round a golden palace within, a palace and castle in one;
Island and ocean beyond; a vision of hills in the west:—
But he pass'd and enter'd the castle; and well they
 welcomed the guest!
Two brothers, gracious and tall as the Twins of Heaven,
 are there,
Prime in their golden youth, and golden-filleted hair;
At the chess they sit, black robed and stately and silent;
 but, O!
Beside them what lily-vision,—no shoot of the lilies that
 grow
In the gardens of earth, but such as of yore at the feet
 of the Maid
Blessed among all women, with angel-adoring was laid!

And as that with its central gold, so She in her ivory
    chair
Crown'd with her golden head, sits queen-like and
    gracious and fair:
And he bow'd to that flower of grace, and trembled; and
    now by her side
He is throned, and he clasps her; and all his heart leaps
    forth to the Bride:—
And the bay of the hounds, with the leashes at strife, on
    his blessedness broke,
And the shields on the lances that jangled and jarr'd;
    and Maxen awoke.

Then to Rome he moved back slowly; his look set idly
    on space;
Seeing not what he saw, for earth had transfigured her
    face:
Love to his soul gave eyes; he knew things are not as
    they seem;
The dream is his real life; the world around him the
    dream.
And he sate in the palace apart, and watch'd the Septen-
    trion star;
Till his senators came around, and buzz'd of tumults and
    war,
Pushing him back into life; and sent their embassy forth

To search for the maid who was hid in that dim love-
    land of the north,
Seek her, his Bride: 'O my Love! and only tell her
    from me
'Let her bid me down from the throne, let her bid me
    over the sea,
'Mountains of yawning chasm, ice-bleeding footsteps and
    torn,
'I follow and yearn for her still, as twilight yearns for the
    morn.'

Then Maximus smiled and spake no more and sank back
    in the dream,
And the heralds arose and set forth on their way,
    ascending the stream.
Twice they went up o'er the mountain, and twice they
    levell'd the plain,
Till they reach'd the fair coast of Arvon, and enter'd the
    castle of Sain.
Gracious and tall as the Twins of Heaven, the brothers
    are there,
Kynan and Adeon, sons of old Eudav, Caradoc's heir:
And there sate the Maid, not that false one whom
    Gwydion fashion'd of flowers,
But sweet and pure, one lily, and worthy of Paradise
    bowers:—

Rose as they came;—not expectant;—yet Nature so
    wrought in her blood
And the subtle force of the dream, she knew the men as
    they stood:
And Love threw his rosy robe o'er the maiden breast and
    the brow,
—For soon doth the gentle heart, O Love! thy lesson
    avow;—
And they hail her 'Empress of Rome,—there Maxen
    awaits his bride,
'Bidding thee rise and come:'—But she, with the
    crimson of pride
'If he loves, he will seek his Love;'—and pass'd from
    the hall with a sigh;
And the heralds abash'd set forth from the gray to the
    sunnier sky.
Twice they rose o'er the mountain, and twice they levell'd
    the plain,
Till they saw the vision of Rome and the Golden Palace
    again.

But when Maximus heard their missive, in wrath he
    blush'd, and he cried
'O brood of slavish courtiers! O base unmannerly pride!
'Is it thus ye would win fair maid? . . . for with softness
    softer than snow

' On her ear the sounds should fall that ask her herself to bestow,
' Sweetest and greatest of gifts! . . . O more than Heaven to me,
' Womanhood all in one maid! The Caesar bows him to thee!'

Then again upstream he journey'd; and when the mountain was nigh,
Dark in the liquid eve, drew bridle and gazed on the sky,
Seeking his guide to the north, one star, and ' Changeless as thou,
'Set in Love's zenith,' he said, 'I follow the dream and the vow;
' Ever follow and find her;' . . . and now, as onward he strode,
'Twas as though in a dream he moved, where of yore he had trodden the road,
And his feet upbore him as wings; for the thought of his heart's desire,
Sweetness ineffable, urged, and the Polestar beckon'd him higher.
And as whose Thessalian steeds at Olympia master the ground,
Steering with rudder-reins and skill the long Stadion round,

'Mid crashing and crossing of wheels, whilst yet the eye
    of the soul,
Seeing the victor wreath, is inwardly rapt on the goal:
So sees he the lily maid; . . . when, lo! on the height
    of the height
The Spirit of Rome, a Goddess in galaxy-radiance bright,
Helm'd and clothed in the awe of the ages, lovely-
    severe,
Breaks forth from the midnight, crying 'O Caesar, what
    doest thou here?
'Shame on a barbarous bride!' and bars the road with
    her lance;
In vain; his heart within him is hot; Love sounds an
    advance.
'O fairest!' he cried, 'But, with thee, for the cave of a
    shepherd I'd quit
'Rome and her heartless pomp, and, with thee, find my
    heaven in it:—
'Full fresh fountains are there, the softness of heather
    and lawn;
'Woods where an age would lapse by thy side, in sweet-
    ness withdrawn:
'Life to its promise true, by its own perfection secure;
'Safety of heart in heart, and love in identity sure.
'O! if otherwise Heaven should will, the life of love be
    denied,

'Better that this once Caesar in wild wood and antre
    should hide;
'Suffer in silence, dream of the dream, an exile unknown,
'Far from the frost of mankind, the golden lie of the
    throne!'
—Thus his heart to his heart, as unswerving he dipp'd
    o'er mountain and plain,
And saw the fair coast of Arvon, the tower'd palace again.

So he enter'd, and all the months that had pass'd, the joy
    and the teen,
The fears and the exultations, were now as they never
    had been;
Moment with moment clasp'd hands; and again he
    beheld them there,
Kynan and Adeon, heirs of old Eudav, Caradoc's heir,
Royal as he was royal; and there, his lily of grace,
Queen in her maiden presence, and all the pure soul in
    the face;
And love, as the tide of spring, in her heart runs rising
    and fast,
Loving because she is loved; and smiling a silent At last!
'Empress of Rome! at thy feet' . . . . Then (for yet
    survived in the blood
Some smack of the saltness of Nature, her healthy primi-
    tive mood),

THE DREAM OF MAXEN WLEDIG 19

As a bridegroom he clasps the maiden of Gwynedd, the
Bride on the throne,
One for life and for death!—the dream and the real are
one!
And soul joins soul in one kiss, a seal of passionate fire;
And Maxen wins, and is won, achieving his heart's desire.

The substance of this piece will be found in Lady C. Guest's admirable translation of the early legends of Wales, 'The Mabin-'ogion.' These tales have a wild magical charm, a remoteness of incident and landscape, to which I know no parallel.

'Maximus,' says the translator, 'the Maxen of the present Tale,
' was invested by his army with the Imperial purple in the year
' 383. He was of low birth, and Spanish origin. He served
' much in Britain, in which island he commanded at the time of
' his elevation.... Maximus is the subject of many Welsh legends.'

Molossian musical roar: The mastiffs of the Molossi, a tribe of Epirus, were famous in the ancient world.

The two horns: Rhenus bicornis: Aen. viii: 727.

Arvon: the western coast of Caernarvonshire, opposite Anglesey. The Wicklow mountains, further west, are occasionally seen from the summit of Snowdon.

Sain: 'They saw Aber Sain, and a castle at the mouth of the ' river.' Caernarvon here seems to have been thought of in the legend.

Gwydion: The tale of the maid, whom Gwydion's magic formed of flowers, is told in the Mabinogi 'Math the son of Mathonwy.' She is faithless to her husband, and Gwydion finally changes her into an owl.

GARIANONUM

GRAY bulwark, that above the marshes gray
Horizon-like along the horizon stands,
Rock-rampart huge, work worthy Roman hands,
    Framed the strong Roman way,

Indurate flint and brick in ruddy tiers,
With immemorial lichen frosted o'er;
Rent by some earthquake-throe perchance of yore,
    Or undergnaw'd by years:—

Life's tide flows once and passes; but o'er thee
Man's generations wave on wave have swept:
—Here first their guard the Imperial eagles kept
    'Gainst native liberty;

Here, in the night of history, Saxon, Dane,
And those stern landlords from the Neustrian coast,
—Three names of one three-headed Northern host,
    Slayers in turn and slain,—

With wide-eyed wonder by the pile might stand,
And touch, and climb, and hold thee for some fort
By Nature moulded in colossal sport,
    Or work of Jotun hand :—

Or some hoar pilgrim-king from Peter's shrine
Here found his Rome beneath another air,
And built his hut within the shelter'd square;
    And saw the gray marsh line,

Green bluffs around, and sinuous streams that go,
E'en as we see them; while the lark on high
Hung o'er the field, and with the same sweet cry
    Fell on his nest below;

And Nature ran her course immutable:
The castle wheatfield ripen'd to the sheaf
Through green to ruddy waves; the elmen leaf
    Thinn'd into gold, and fell

And moulder'd,—as we moulder:—O brief race
Of man! O toy of Nature! whom the oak
O'erlives, that lives to earn the woodman's stroke;
    Who sees his little space

Of being by the raven's years o'erpass'd,
Or the green babbler of the blazing Line:—

While nations rise and blossom and decline,
   And these strong bulwarks last

Outbraving creeds and dynasties and chiefs
And hearts of men and women, that once beat
Numerous past number, each a world complete
   Of loves and hopes and griefs,

Now cold as yon gray flint-wall, which the breath
Of Autumn tear-dews,—as though morn by morn
Earth wept the souls that must this day be born,
   Sacred from birth, to death!

Mysterious law! Sad irony of Fate!
Lo, this brute matter, lowest on the file
Of Being, unselfconscious, heartless, vile,—
   Yet framed for longer date

Than we!—The tree its century has; the flower
Its summer; their brief annals beast and bird;
The torrent dries and is no longer heard;
   Imperial Man his hour

Of aspiration, knowledge, love, and faith,
Has, and has not, almost before he has;
And all his stores of viewless treasure pass
   Behind the cloud of death!

—And yet he is avenged, Imperial Man !
Enormous Nature feels through all her sway
The chronic progress of a slow decay
    Deep-rooted in her plan.

Of balanced force in equable array,
Maintaining all the worlds in order sure,
Eternal compensations, that secure
    Each star his changeless way,

The sages told :—Not so !—The doom of earth
Was set ere first her living freight she bore :
The eternal worm was gnawing at the core
    Of all things from their birth.

The sun devours the sky : the meteor-showers
Strike, and exhaust their impulse, feeding him :
The eddying star-dust wreaths through space that
        swim
    Lapse into lower powers

And energies less vital :—Earth her pace,
Soft daily turning, age on age delays,
Braked by the tides, and lengthens out the days,
    And in the moon's dead face,

Intolerable white, volcano-starr'd,
Reads her own fate :—how from her orb must go

Life, verdure, air; all things that move and flow
    Burnt utterly off and scarr'd.

Then round a dying sun awhile will roll
The dull, dead earth, accomplishing her doom;
Half stony glare, half ever-freezing gloom,
    Vacant of life and soul:—

Yet on her outworn surface bearing round
Perchance, with rocks and plains and dwindling seas,
Some sign of the lost race,—some walls like these,
    With flint-work iron-bound;

Gray towers and gables; roads through mountains hew'd;
Outlines of cities, crumbling in their sleep;
—Such as in Equatorial forests deep
    The wayfarer has view'd

Crying, What vanish'd race these regions trod?—
—But none will be to ask our history then:
Silence and death:—the busy tribes of men
    Gather'd to rest and God.

Garianonum, now Burgh Castle, is a large fortified camp in Suffolk, placed near the point where the Waveney flows into the Yare. The original foundation has been assigned to Ostorius Scapula, in A.D. 46 : but the structure now standing (640 feet long by 370 broad) indicates a much later date in the Roman occupation of Britain.

Fursaeus, an Irish monk, who came to East Anglia during the reign of Sigebert, cir. 640, built within the camp a monastery, and appears to have persuaded the king to retire also into monastic life. Whilst at Burgh, in a trance he is said to have seen certain visions anticipatory of Dante's *Divina Commedia*: (*Bede*, B. III : ch. xix).

The doom of earth: I have here attempted to render the impressive arguments of Sir W. Thomson and of Helmholtz on the time-limits of the earth's rotation. The effect of the tides—the 'friction 'brake,' as it has been named—was first pointed out by Immanuel Kant. Helmholtz, however, does not even admit for mankind that longer duration which we might anticipate if the race were to be destroyed only by the inevitable and ever progressing exhaustion of active energy. The same forces which produced former geological revolutions will, he thinks, 'more probably bring about the last day ' of the human race than those distant cosmical alterations.' (*Popular Lectures, First Series.*)

The sun devours the sky: compare Lucretius, V : 380-5.

Star-dust wreaths: Nebulae.

PAULINUS AND EDWIN

627

The black-hair'd gaunt Paulinus
   By ruddy Edwin stood:—
'Bow down, O King of Deira,
   'Before the holy Rood!
'Cast forth thy demon idols,
   'And worship Christ our Lord!'
—But Edwin look'd and ponder'd,
   And answer'd not a word.

Again the gaunt Paulinus
   To ruddy Edwin spake:
'God offers life immortal
   'For his dear Son's own sake!
'Wilt thou not hear his message
   'Who bears the Keys and Sword?'
—But Edwin look'd and ponder'd,
   And answer'd not a word.

Rose then a sage old warrior;
   Was five-score winters old;
Whose beard from chin to girdle
   Like one long snow-wreath roll'd :—
' At Yule-time in our chamber
   ' We sit in warmth and light,
' While cavern-black around us
   ' Lies the grim mouth of Night.

' Athwart the room a sparrow
   ' Darts from the open door :
' Within the happy hearth-light
   ' One red flash,—and no more !
' We see it born from darkness,
   ' And into darkness go :—
' So is our life, King Edwin !
   ' Ah, that it should be so !

' But if this pale Paulinus
   ' Have somewhat more to tell ;
' Some news of whence and whither,
   ' And where the Soul may dwell :—
' If on that outer darkness
   ' The sun of Hope may shine ;—
' He makes life worth the living !
   ' I take his God for mine !'

So spake the wise old warrior ;
And all about him cried
'Paulinus' God hath conquer'd !
'And he shall be our guide :—
'For he makes life worth living,
'Who brings this message plain,—
'When our brief days are over,
'That we shall live again.'

    Paulinus was one of the four missionaries sent from Rome by Gregory the Great in 601. The marriage of Edwin, King of Northumbria, with Ethelburga, sister to Eadbald of Kent, opened Paulinus's way to northern England. Bede, born less than fifty years after, has given an admirable narrative of Edwin's conversion : which is very completely told in Bright's *Early English Church History*, B. IV.

ALFRED THE GREAT

849-901

I

THE Isle of Roses in her Lindian shrine,
   Athena's dwelling, gleam'd with golden song
   Of Pindar, set in gold the walls along,
Blazoning the praise of Héraclés divine.
—O Poets, who for us have wrought the mine
   Of old Romance, illusive pearl and gold,
   Its star-fair maids, knights of heroic mould,
Ye lend the rays that on their features shine,

Ideal strength and beauty:—But O thou
Fair Truth!—to thee with deeper faith we bow;
   Knowing thy genuine heroes bring with them
Their more than poetry: From these we learn
What man can be: By their own light they burn
   As in far heavens the Pleiad diadem.

II

The fair-hair'd boy is at his mother's knee,
   A many-colour'd page before them spread,
   Gay summer harvest-field of gold and red,
With lines and staves of ancient minstrelsy.

But through her eyes alone the child can see,
    From her sweet lips partake the words of song,
    And looks as one who feels a hidden wrong,
Or gazes on some feat of gramarye.

'When thou canst use it, thine the book!' she cried:
He blush'd, and clasp'd it to his breast with pride:—
    'Unkingly task!' his comrades cry; In vain;
All work ennobles nobleness, all art,
He sees; Head governs hand; and in his heart
    All knowledge for his province he has ta'en.

III

Few the bright days, and brief the fruitful rest,
    As summer-clouds that o'er the valley flit:—
    To other tasks his genius he must fit;
The Dane is in the land, uneasy guest!
—O sacred Athelney, from pagan quest
    Secure, sole haven for the faithful boy
    Waiting God's issue with heroic joy
And unrelaxing purpose in the breast!

The Dragon and the Raven, inch by inch,
For England fight; nor Dane nor Saxon flinch;
    Then Alfred strikes his blow; the realm is free:—
He, changing at the font his foe to friend,
Yields for the time, to gain the far-off end,
    By moderation doubling victory.

IV

O much-vex'd life, for us too short, too dear!
   The laggard body lame behind the soul;
   Pain, that ne'er marr'd the mind's serene control;
Breathing on earth heaven's aether atmosphere,
God with thee, and the love that casts out fear!
   A soul in life's salt ocean guarding sure
   The freshness of youth's fountain sweet and pure,
And to all natural impulse crystal-clear :—

To service or command, to low and high
Equal at once in magnanimity,
   The Great by right divine thou only art!
Fair star, that crowns the front of England's morn,
Royal with Nature's royalty inborn,
   And English to the very heart of heart!

The Isle of Roses: The Rhodians engraved Pindar's Seventh Olympian Ode in golden letters within the temple of the Lindian Athene.

The fair-hair'd boy: There is a singular unanimity among historians in regard to this 'darling of the English,' whose life has been vividly sketched by Freeman (*Conquest*, ch. ii); by Green (*English People*, B. I : ch. iii); and, earlier, by my Father in his short *History of the Anglo-Saxons*, ch. vi-viii.

Changing at the font: Alfred was godfather to Guthrun the Dane, when baptized after his defeat at Ethandune in 878.

To service or command: Compare Aristotle's splendid description of the 'great-souled man' : *Nic. Eth.* IV : iii.

A DANISH BARROW

on the East Devon coast

LIE still, old Dane, below thy heap!
　—A sturdy-back and sturdy-limb,
　Whoe'er he was, I warrant him
Upon whose mound the single sheep
　Browses and tinkles in the sun,
　Within the narrow vale alone.

Lie still, old Dane! This restful scene
　Suits well thy centuries of sleep:
　The soft brown roots above thee creep,
The lotus flaunts his ruddy sheen,
　And,—vain memento of the spot,—
　The turquoise-eyed forget-me-not.

Lie still!—Thy mother-land herself
　Would know thee not again: no more
　The Raven from the northern shore
Hails the bold crew to push for pelf,
　Through fire and blood and slaughter'd kings,
　'Neath the black terror of his wings.

And thou,—thy very name is lost!
    The peasant only knows that here
    Bold Alfred scoop'd thy flinty bier,
And pray'd a foeman's prayer, and tost
    His auburn head, and said 'One more
    'Of England's foes guards England's shore,'

And turn'd and pass'd to other feats,
    And left thee in thine iron robe,
    To circle with the circling globe,
While Time's corrosive dewdrop eats
    The giant warrior to a crust
    Of earth in earth, and rust in rust.

So lie: and let the children play
    And sit like flowers upon thy grave
    And crown with flowers,—that hardly have
A briefer blooming-tide than they;—
    By hurrying years urged on to rest,
    As thou, within the Mother's breast.

HASTINGS

October 14 : 1066

'GYRTH, is it dawn in the sky that I see? or is all the
      sky blood?
'Heavy and sore was the fight in the North: yet we
      fought for the good.
'O but—Brother 'gainst brother!—'twas hard!—Now I
      come with a will
'To baste the false bastard of France, the hide of the
      tanyard and mill!
      'Now on the razor-edge lies
      'England the precious, the prize!
'God aiding, the Raven at Stamford we smote;
'One more stroke for the land here I strike and devote!'

Red with fresh breath on her lips came the dawn; and
      Harold uprose;
Kneels as man before God; then takes his long pole-axe,
      and goes
Where round their woven wall, tough ash-palisado, they
      crowd;
Mightily cleaves and binds, to his comrades crying aloud

'Englishmen stalwart and true,
'But one word has Harold for you!
'When from the field the false foreigners run,
'Stand firm in your castle, and all will be won!

'Now, with God o'er us, and Holy Rood, arm!'—And
he ran for his spear:
But Gyrth held him back, 'mong his brothers Gyrth the
most honour'd, most dear:
'Go not, Harold! thine oath is against thee! the Saints
look askance:
'I am not king; let me lead them, me only: mine be
the chance!'
—'No! The leader must lead!
'Better that Harold should bleed!
'To the souls I appeal, not the dust of the tomb:—
'King chosen of Edward and England, I come!'

Over Heathland surge banners and lances, three armies;
William the last,
Grasping his mace; Rome's gonfanon round him Rome's
majesty cast:
O'er his Bretons Fergant, o'er the hireling squadrons
Montgomery lords,
Jerkin'd archers, and mail-clads, and horsemen with pennons and swords:—

—England, in threefold array,
Anchor, and hold them at bay,
Firm set in your own wooden walls; and the wave
Of high-crested Frenchmen will break on their grave.

So to the palisade on! There, Harold and Leofwine and
　　　　　Gyrth
Stand like a triple Thor, true brethren in arms as in birth:
And above the fierce standards strain at their poles as
　　　　　they stream on the gale;
One, the old Dragon of Wessex, and one, a Warrior in
　　　　　mail.
　　　'God Almighty!' they cry!
　　　'Haro!' the Northmen reply:—
As when eagles are gather'd and loud o'er the prey,
Shout! for 'tis England the prize of the fray!

And as when two lightning-clouds tilt, between them an
　　　　　arrowy sleet
Hisses and darts; till the challenging thunders are heard,
　　　　　and they meet;
Across fly javelins and serpents of flame: green earth and
　　　　　blue sky
Mix'd in the dim tornado:—so now the battle goes
　　　　　high.
　　　Shearing through helmet and limb
　　　Glaive-steel and battle-axe grim:

As the flash of the reaper in summer's high wheat,
King Harold cleaves horseman and horse at his feet.

O vainly the whirlwind of France up the turf to the
    palisade swept:
Shoulder to shoulder the Englishmen stand, and the
    shield-wall is kept :—
As, in a summer to be, when England and she yet again
Strove for the sovereignty, firm stood our squares, through
    the pitiless rain
    Death rain'd o'er them all day;
    —Happier, not braver than they
Who e'en yet on Senlac their still garrison keep,
Sleeping a long Marathonian sleep!

'Madmen, why turn?' cried the Duke,—for the horse-
    men recoil from the slope;
'Behold me! I live!'—and he lifted the ventayle;
    'before you is hope:
'Death, not safety, behind!'—and he spurs to the centre
    once more,
Lion-like leaps on the standard and Harold : but Gyrth
    is before!
    'Down! He is down!' is the shout:
    'On with the axes! Out, Out!'
—He rises again : the mace circles its stroke,
And falls as the thunderbolt falls on the oak.

—Gyrth is crush'd, and Leofwine is crush'd; yet the
shields hold their wall:
'Edith alone of my dear ones is left me, and dearest of
all!
'Edith has said she would seek me to-day when the battle
is done;
'Her love more precious alone than kingdoms and victory
won:
'O for the sweetness of home!
'O for the kindness to come!'
Then around him again the wild war-dragons roar,
And he drinks the keen draught of the battle once
more.

—'Anyhow from their rampart to lure them, to shatter
the bucklers and wall,
'Acting a flight,' in his craft thought William, and sign'd
to recall
His left battle:—O countrymen! slow to be roused!
roused, always, as then,
Reckless of life or death, bent only to quit you like
men!—
As bolts from the bow-string they go,
Whirl them and hurl them below,
Where the deep foss yawns for the foe in his course,
Piled up and brimming with horseman and horse.

As when October's sun, long caught in a curtain of
    gray,
With a flood of impatient crimson breaks out, at the
    dying of day,
And trees and green fields, the hills and the skies, are all
    steep'd in the stain;—
So o'er the English one hope flared forth, one moment,—
    in vain!
    As hail when the corn-fields are deep,
    Down the fierce arrow-points sweep:
Now the basnets of France o'er the palisade frown;
The shield-fort is shatter'd; the Dragon is down.

O then there was dashing and dinting of axe and of
    broadsword and spear:
Blood crying out to blood: and Hatred that casteth out
    fear!
Loud where the fight is the loudest, the slaughter-breath
    hot in the air,
O what a cry was that!—the cry of a nation's de-
    spair!
    —Hew down the best of the land!
    Down them with mace and with brand!
The fell foreign arrow has crash'd to the brain;
England with Harold the Englishman slain!

Yet they fought on for their England! of ineffaceable
fame
Worthy, and stood to the death, though the greedy sword,
like a flame,
Bit and bit yet again in the solid ranks, and the dead
Heap where they die, and hills of foemen about them are
spread:—
—Hew down the best of the land,
There, to a man, where they stand!
Till, kindly-remorseful, in silence again
Night veils the red hillside, and weeps for the slain.

Heroes unburied, unwept!—But a wan gray thing in the
night
Like a marsh-wisp flits to and fro through the blood-lake,
the steam of the fight;
Turning the bodies, exploring the features with delicate
touch;
Stumbling as one that finds nothing: but now!—as one
finding too much:
Love through mid-midnight will see:
Edith the fair! It is he!
Clasp him once more, the heroic, the dear:
Harold was England: and Harold lies here.

This battle, incontestably the most critical of the many battles fought in these islands, is admirably described, with the detail which its importance demands, and a map, to which I specially refer readers, in Freeman's *History of the Norman Conquest*. A brief but brilliant narration is given in my Father's short early history.

The hide of the tanyard: See the story of Arlette or Herleva, the tanner's daughter, mother to William 'the Bastard.'

At Stamford: At Stamford Bridge, over the Derwent, Harold defeated his brother Tostig and Harold Hardrada, 25th Sept. 1066.

Your castle: Harold's triple palisade upon the hill of battle is called *quasi castellum* in a passage quoted by Freeman from Henry of Huntingdon.

Gyrth held him back: The credibility of the legends on this point is, however, more than questioned by Freeman.

Rome's gonfanon: 'The consecrated banner, the gift of Rome ' and of Hildebrand': (*Freeman*).

The twin standards: These were planted on the spot chosen for the high-altar of the Abbey of Battle. The *Warrior* was Harold's ' personal ensign.'

Harold cleaves horseman: The long-handled axe, wielded with both hands, was introduced by Cnut, 'but was probably made ' more distinctly the national weapon by Harold': (*Freeman*).

The ventayle: Used here for the *nasale* or nose-piece shown in the Bayeux Tapestry.

DEATH IN THE FOREST

August 2 : 1100

WHERE the greenwood is greenest
At gloaming of day,
Where the twelve-antler'd stag
Faces boldest at bay;
Where the solitude deepens,
Till almost you hear
The blood-beat of the heart
As the quarry slips near;
His comrades outridden
With scorn in the race,
The Red King is hallooing
His hounds to the chase.

What though the Wild Hunt
Like a whirlwind of hell
Yestereve ran the forest,
With baying and yell :—
In his cups the Red heathen
Mocks God to the face;
—'In the devil's name, shoot;
Tyrrell, ho !—to the chase !'

—Now with worms for his courtiers
He lies in the narrow
Cold couch of the chancel!
—But whence was the arrow?

The dread vision of Serlo
That call'd him to die,
The true dreams of the morning
In vain have gone by.
The blood of young Richard
Cries on him in vain,
In the heart of the Lindwood
By arbalest slain.
And he plunges alone
In the Serpent-glade gloom,
As one whom the Furies
Hound headlong to doom.

His sin goes before him,
The lust and the pride;
And the curses of England
Breathe hot at his side.
And the Evil-wood walls
That in ashes were laid
For his jest and his pleasure,
Frown black o'er the glade:—

—Now with worms for his courtiers
He lies in the narrow
Cold couch of the chancel!
—But whence was the arrow?

Then a shudder of death
Flicker'd fast through the wood :—
And they found the Red King
Red-gilt in his blood.
What wells up in his throat?
Is it cursing, or prayer?
Was it Henry, or Tyrrell,
Or demon, who there
Has dyed the fell tyrant
Twice crimson in gore,
While the soul disembodied
Hunts on to hell-door?

—Ah! friendless in death!
Rude forest-hands fling
On the charcoaler's wain
What but now was the king!
And through the long Minster
The carcass they bear,
And huddle it down
Without priest, without prayer :—

Now with worms for his courtiers
He lies in the narrow
Cold couch of the chancel!
—But whence was the arrow?

In his cups: Rufus, it is said, was 'fey,' as the old phrase has it, on the day of his death. He feasted long and high, and then chose out two cross-bow shafts, presenting them to Tyrrell with the exclamation given above.

The vision of Serlo: He was Abbot of Gloucester, and had sent to Rufus the narrative of an ominous dream, reported in the Monastery.

The true dreams: On his last night Rufus 'laid himself down
' to sleep, but not in peace; the attendants were startled by the
' King's voice—a bitter cry—a cry for help—a cry for deliverance—
' he had been suddenly awakened by a dreadful dream, as of
' exquisite anguish befalling him in that ruined church, at the foot
' of the Malwood rampart.' Palgrave: *Hist. of Normandy and of England*, B. IV: ch. xii.

Young Richard: Son to Robert Courthose, and hunting, as his uncle's guest, in the New Forest in May 1100, was mysteriously slain by a heavy bolt from a Norman Arbalest.

The Evil-wood walls: 'Amongst the sixty churches which had
' been ruined,' my Father remarks, in his notice of the New Forest,
' the sanctuary below the mystic Malwood was peculiarly remark-
' able. . . . You reach the Malwood easily from the Leafy Lodge
' in the favourite deer-walk, the Lind-hurst, the Dragon's wood.'

Through the long Minster: Winchester. Rufus, with much hesitation, was buried in the chancel as a king; but no religious service or ceremonial was celebrated:—'All men thought that
' prayers were hopeless.'

EDITH OF ENGLAND

1100

THROUGH sapling shades of summer green,
  By glade and height and hollow,
Where Rufus rode the stag to bay,
King Henry spurs a jocund way,
  Another chase to follow.
But when he came to Romsey gate
  The doors are open'd free,
And through the gate like sunshine streams
  A maiden company:—
One girdled with the vervain-red,
  And three in sendal gray,
And touch the trembling rebeck-strings
  To their soft roundelay;—

  —The bravest knight may fail in fight;
    The red rust edge the sword;
  The king his crown in dust lay down;
    But Love is always Lord!

King Henry at her feet flings down,
  His helmet ringing loudly:—

His kisses worship Edith's hand;
'Wilt thou be Queen of all the land?'
 —O red she blush'd and proudly!
Red as the crimson girdle bound
 Beneath her gracious breast;
Red as the silken scarf that flames
 Above his lion-crest.
She lifts and casts the cloister-veil
 All on the cloister-floor:—
The novice maids of Romsey smile,
 And think of love once more.

'Well, well, to blush!' the Abbess cried,
 'The veil and vow deriding
'That rescued thee, in baby days,
'From insolence of Norman gaze,
 'In pure and holy hiding.
'—O royal child of South and North,
 'Malcolm and Margaret,
'The promised bride of Heaven art thou,
 'And Heaven will not forget!
'What recks it, if an alien King
 'Encoronet thy brow,
'Or if the false Italian priest
 'Pretend to loose the vow?'

O then to white the red rose went
  On Edith's cheek abiding!
With even glance she answer'd meek
'I leave the life I did not seek,
  'In holy Church confiding.'
And then she look'd on Henry's face,
  And Anselm join'd the hands
That in one race two races bound
  By everlasting bands.
So Love is Lord, and Alfred's blood
  Returns the land to sway;
And all her happy maidens join
  In their soft roundelay:

—For though the knight may fail in fight,
  The red rust edge the sword,
The king his crown in dust lay down,
  Yet Love is always Lord!

Edith, (who, after marriage, took the name Matilda in compliment to Henry's mother,) daughter to Malcolm King of Scotland by Margaret, granddaughter of Edmund Ironside, had been brought up by her aunt Christina, and placed in Romsey Abbey, apparently after Margaret's death in 1093, for security against Norman violence. But she had always refused to take the vows, and was hence, in opposition to her aunt's wish, declared canonically free to marry by Anselm; called here an *Italian priest*, as born at Aosta. The marriage was on Nov. 11, 1100, but the wooing appears to have been taken in hand by Henry, who had been long attached to the Princess, at once upon his accession.

LE CHATEAU GAILLARD

1199

Fair land of breezy hill and open plain,
  Wealth of green herb and grain,
Orchards that o'er white bluff and river-wall
  Come rounding, while the stream
Upon its silver takes a golden gleam,
Or seaward floats the ruddy globes that fall:—

Fair land of Rollo and of him, once lord
  Of England by the sword;
Fair Seine, that flashest from Les Andelys
  Toward thy first bridling bridge
At Rouen, and beneath its chalky ridge
Redoublest Castle Gaillard, to the sea

Dimpling in fullness:—not without a sigh
  The Englishman goes by!
This richer, broader, realm; this sun-steep'd land
  Was England once, we say;—
—Vain half-regret!—For Nature held her way,
Modelling each race in its own strength to stand:

Each its perfected genius to the store
   Of world's wealth giving o'er;
Teachers and learners in a peaceful strife;
   Not merged in one, the scheme
Of theorists in their cosmopolitan dream,
Yet all co-operant for the higher life;

Each being most for all, when most itself;
   Scorning the ignoble pelf
Of conquest,—the mean jealousies that eye
   Another's weal askance,
Or 'neath a neighbour's frailty mask advance,
And compass suicide by victory.

—O wisdom that the nations will not read
   Through centuries of greed,
From Gaillard built, to Metz annex'd! . . . For thou,
   In blind defiant pride
By Richard named, when o'er Seine's silver tide
He saw his Saucy Castle crown the brow,

Than rock more rock-like:—In one magic year
   Thy walls their mass uprear;
A bastion'd cliff,—enormous strength!—toward France
   A challenge for the crown,
Gage of defiance, Richard throws thee down,
Beyond this bound the Lion bars advance! . . .

Vain insolence of the sword! Vain hope, the tide
    By force to set aside
Severing two peoples by one narrow sea;
    To lay the surging flood
When races feel the impulse of the blood,
The unconquerable instinct to be free,

To be themselves!—Fair France, our gallant foe,
    To thee a debt we owe,
A late repentance for ancestral wrong,—
    Not that first strife, when we
Were one with France, Plantagenet Henry's fee,
But those gay triumphs which yet shine in song,

While our brave hearts their lives at Azincourt,
    Poitiers, and Creçy, pour,
—Crime-follies, if heroic!—Our grim lord,
    William, with iron hand,
First forged in one this long-divided land
By that Thor's hammer of his conquering sword:—

Then the two races fused, and, conquest o'er,
    Heart beat with heart once more:—
Yet England was not genuine England, true
    To her own self alone,
Till within seas was fix'd her lordly throne,
Imperial emerald set in zoning blue.

—Survivor of thyself!—in noontide blaze
   On Gaillard's height we gaze,
Drifting against light clouds that flit and go;
   And watch the shadow creep
From bastion over bastion on thy keep,
While sudden lightnings flash from Seine below;—

While pimpernel beneath the heaven's clear dome
   Stars forth its coral bloom,
And agrimony breathes her citron balm;
   And that huge tower above
Sleeps in the peace of sunshine, and the dove
Broods crooning o'er her nest, and all is calm.

    This castle was built by Richard to bridle and secure Normandy, as a kind of fortified outwork to Rouen. 'As a monument of 'warlike skill his *Saucy Castle*, Chateau Gaillard, stands first 'among the fortresses of the Middle Ages. Richard fixed its site 'where the Seine bends suddenly at Gaillon in a great semicircle, 'and where the valley of Les Andelys breaks the line of the chalk 'cliffs along its banks. . . . Even now in its ruin we can under- 'stand the triumphant outburst of its royal builder as he saw it 'rising against the sky, *How pretty a child is mine, this child of but* '*one year old!*' (*Green*, B. II : ch. iv).

    That Thor's hammer: 'Instead of crushing England,' says Green, 'the Conquest did more than any event that had gone before to 'build up an English people. All local distinctions died away 'beneath the common presence of the stranger': (B. III : ch. i).

A CRUSADER'S TOMB

1230

UNNAMED, unknown :—his hands across his breast
    Set in sepulchral rest,
In yon low cave-like niche the warrior lies,
    —A shrine within a shrine,—
Full of gray peace, while day to darkness dies.

Then the forgotten dead at midnight come
    And throng their chieftain's tomb,
Murmuring the toils o'er which they toil'd, alive,
    The feats of sword and love;
And all the air thrills like a summer hive.

—How so! thou say'st!—This is the poet's right!
    He looks with larger sight
Than they who hedge their view by present things,
    The small, parochial world
Of sight and touch: and what he sees, he sings.

The steel-shell'd host, that, gleaming as it turns,
    Like autumn lightning burns,

One moment's azure; the fresh flags that glance
    As cornflowers o'er the corn,
Till war's stern step show'd like a gala dance,

He also sees; and pierces to the heart,
    Scanning the genuine part
Each Red-Cross pilgrim plays: Some, gold-enticed;
    By love or lust or fame
Urged; or who yearn to kiss the grave of Christ

And find their own, life-wearied:—Motley band!
    O! ere they quit the Land
How maim'd, how marr'd, how changed from all that pride
    In which so late they left
Orwell or Thames, with sails out-swelling wide

And music tuneable with the timing oar
    Clear heard from shore to shore;
All Europe streaming to the mystic East!
    —Now on their sun-smit ranks
The dusky squadrons close in vulture-feast,

And that fierce Day-star's blazing ball their sight
    Sears with excess of light;
Or through dun sand-clouds the blue scimitar's edge
    Slopes down like fire from heaven,
Mowing them as the thatcher mows the sedge.

Then many a heart remember'd, as the skies
    Grew dark on dying eyes,
Sweet England; her fresh fields and gardens trim;
    Her tree-embower'd halls;
And the one face that was the world to him.

—And one who fought his fight and held his way,
    Through life's long latter day
Moving among the green, green English meads,
    Ere in this niche he took
His rest, oft 'mid his kinsfolk told the deeds

Of that gay passage through the Midland sea;
    Cyprus and Sicily;
And how the Lion-Heart o'er the Moslem host
    Triumph'd in Ascalon
Or Acre, by the tideless Tyrian coast,

Yet never saw the vast Imperial dome,
    Nor the thrice-holy Tomb :—
—As that great vision of the hidden Grail
    By bravest knights of old
Unseen :—seen only of pure Parcivale.

The 'Third Crusade,' 1189-1193, is the subject of this poem. Richard Coeur de Lion carried his followers by way of Sicily and Cyprus: making a transient conquest of the latter. In the Holy

Land the siege of Acre consumed the time and strength of the Crusaders. They suffered terribly in the wilderness of Mount Carmel, and when at last preparing to march on Jerusalem (1192) were recalled to Ascalon. Richard now advanced to Bethany, but was unable to reach the Holy City. The tale is that while riding with a party of knights one of them called out, 'This way, my lord, and 'you will see Jerusalem.' But Richard hid his face and said, 'Alas! '—they who are not worthy to win the Holy City are not worthy to 'behold it.'

The vast Imperial dome : The Church of the Holy Sepulchre was built by the Emperor Constantine; A.D. 326-335.

The hidden Grail : This vision forms the subject of one of A. Tennyson's noblest *Idylls*.

A BALLAD OF EVESHAM

1265

EARL Simon on the Abbey tower
In summer sunshine stood,
While helm and lance o'er Greenhill heights
Come glinting through the wood.
'My son!' he cried, 'I know his flag
'Amongst a thousand glancing':—
Fond father! no!—'tis Edward stern
In royal strength advancing.

The Prince fell on him like a hawk
At Al'ster yester-eve,
And flaunts his captured banner now
And flaunts but to deceive:—
—Look round! for Mortimer is by,
And guards the rearward river:—
The hour that parted sire and son
Has parted them for ever!

'Young Simon's dead,' he thinks, and look'd
Upon his living son:
'Now God have mercy on our souls,
'Our bodies are undone!

'But, Hugh and Henry, ye can fly
'Before their bowmen smite us:—
'They come on well! But 'tis from me
'They learn'd the skill to fight us.'

—'For England's cause, and England's laws,
'With you we fight and fall!'
—'Together, then, and die like men,
'And Heaven will hold us all!'
—Then, face to face, and limb to limb,
And sword with sword inwoven,
That stubborn courage of the race
On Evesham field was proven.

O happy hills! O summer sky
Above the valley bent!
Your peacefulness rebukes the rage
Of blood on blood intent!
No thought was then for death or life
Through that long dreadful hour,
While Simon 'mid his faithful few
Stood like an iron tower,

'Gainst which the winds and waves are hurl'd
In vain, unmoved, foursquare;
And round him storm'd the raging swords
Of Edward and De Clare:

And round him in the narrow combe
His white-cross comrades rally,
While ghastly gashings cloud the beck
And crimson all the valley,

And triple sword-thrusts meet his sword,
And thrice the charge he foils,
Though now in threefold flood the foe
Round those devoted boils :
And still the light of England's cause
And England's love was o'er him,
Until he saw his gallant boy
Go down in blood before him :—

He hove his huge two-handed blade,
He cried ' 'Tis time to die ! '
And smote about him like a flail,
And clear'd a space to lie :—
' Thank God ! ' he said ; nor long could life
From loved and lost divide him :—
And night fell o'er De Montfort dead,
And England wept beside him.

In the words given here to Simon (and, indeed, in the bulk of my narrative) I have almost literally followed Prothero's *Life*. The struggle, like other critical conflicts in the days of unprofessional war, was very brief.

THE DIRGE OF LLYWELYN

December 10 : 1282

LLANYNIS on Irvon, thine oaks in the drear
Red eve of December are wind-swept and sere,
Where a king by the stream in his agony lies,
And the life of a land ebbs away as he dies.

O strange, the great sceptre from Caradoc kept
Should pass like the ripple, unhonour'd, unwept!
Unknowing the lance, and the victim unknown,
Far from Aberfraw's halls and Craig Eryri lone!

O dark day of winter and Cambria's shame,
To the treason of Builth when from Gwynedd he came,
And Walwyn and Frankton and Mortimer fell
Closed round unawares by the ford in the dell!

—As who, where the shadow beneath him is thrown,
By some well in Saharan high noontide alone
Sits under the palm-tree, nor hears the low breath
Of the russet-maned foe panting hot for his death;

THE DIRGE OF LLYWELYN

So Llywelyn,—unarm'd, unaware:—Is it she,
Bright star of his morning, when Gwynedd was free,
Fair bride, the long sought, taken early, goes by?
In the heart of the breeze the lost Eleanor's sigh?

Or the one little daughter's sweet face with a gleam
Of glamour looks out, as the dream in a dream?
Or for childhood's first sunshine and calm does he yearn,
As the days of Maesmynan in memory return?

Or,—dear to the heart's-blood as first-love or wife,—
The mountains whose freedom was one with his life,
The gray farms, the green vales of that ancient domain,
The thousand-years' kingdom, he dreams of again?

Or is it the rage of stark Edward; the base
Unkingly revenge on a kinglier race;
The wrong idly wrought on the patriot dead;
The dark castle of doom; the scorn-diadem'd head?

—Lo, where Rodri and Owain await thee!—The foe
Slips nearing in silence: one flash—and one blow!
And the ripple that passes wafts down to the Wye
The last prayer of Llywelyn, the nation's last sigh.

But Llanynis yet sees the white rivulet gleam,
And the leaf of December fall sere on the stream;
While Irvon his dirge whispers on through the combe,
And the purple-topt hills gather round in their gloom.

Where a king: see Appendix.

Aberfraw: in Anglesea: the residence of the royal line of Gwynedd from the time of Rodri Mawr onwards.

Craig Eryri: the Eagle's rock: a name for Snowdon. The bird has been seen in the neighbourhood within late years.

Is it she: Eleanor, daughter to Simon de Montfort. After some years of betrothal and impediment arising from the jealousy of Edward I, she and Llywelyn were married in 1278. But after only two years of happiness, Eleanor died, leaving one child, Catharine.

Maesmynan: by Caerwys in Flintshire; where Llywelyn lived retiredly in youth.

The thousand-years' kingdom: the descent of the royal house of North Wales is legendarily traced from Caradoc-Caractacus. But the accepted genealogy of the Princes of Gwynedd begins with Cunedda Wledig (Paramount) A.D. 346: ending 1282 with Llywelyn son of Gruffyd.

This family is now represented in chief by the house of Wynnstay. They bear the arms traditionally ascribed to Owain Gwynedd: *Vert,* three Eagles displayed in fess, *or;* with the motto *Eryr Eryrod Eryri,* 'an Eagle of the Eagles of Snowdon.'—But Owain enjoys a less doubtful blazon in the splendid couplets of Gray.

Rodri and Owain: Rodri Mawr, (843), who united under his supremacy the other Welsh principalities, Powys and Dinevawr; Owain Gwynedd, (1137),—are among the most conspicuous of Llywelyn's royal predecessors.

THE REJOICING OF THE LAND

1295

So the land had rest! and the cloud of that heart-sore struggle and pain
Rose from her ancient hills, and peace shone o'er her again,
Sunlike chasing the plagues wherewith the land was defiled;
And the leprosy fled, and her flesh came again, as the flesh of a child.

—They were stern and stark, the three children of Rolf, the first from Anjou:
For their own sake loving the land, mayhap, but loving her true:
France the wife, and England the handmaid; yet over the realm
Their eyes were in every place, their hands gripp'd firm on the helm.
Villein and earl, the cowl and the plume, they were bridled alike;

One law for all, but arm'd law,—not swifter to aid than to strike.
Lo, in the twilight transept, the holy places of God,
Not with sunset the steps of the altar are dyed, but with scarlet of blood!
Clang of iron-shod feet, and sheep for their shepherd who cry;
Curses of bestial rage, and proud resolution to die!
—Bare thy own back to the smiter, O king, at the shrine of the dead:
Thy friend thou hast slain in thy folly; the blood of the Saint on thy head:
Proud and priestly, thou say'st;—yet tender and faithful and pure;
True man, and so, true saint;—the crown of his martyrdom sure:—
As friend with his friend, he could brave thee and warn; thou hast silenced the voice,
Ne'er to be heard again :—nor again will Henry rejoice!
Green Erin may yield her, fair Scotland submit; but his sunshine is o'er;
The tooth of the serpent, the child of his bosom, has smote him so sore:—
Like a wolf from the hounds he dragg'd off to his lair, not turning to bay:—
Crying 'shame on a conquer'd king!'—the grim ghost fled sullen away.

Then, as in gray Autumn the heavens are pour'd on the rifted hillside,
When the Rain-stars mistily gleam, and torrents leap white in their pride,
And the valley is all one lake, and the late, unharvested shocks
Are rapt to the sea, the dwellings of man, the red kine and the flocks,—
O'er England the ramparts of law, the old landmarks of liberty fell,
As the brothers in blood and in lust, twin hydra begotten of hell,
Suck'd all the life of the land to themselves, like Lofoden in flood,
One in his pride, in his subtlety one, mocking England and God.
Then once, once only, we knew what tyranny was!—and the stain
Went crimson and black through the soul of the land, for all time, not in vain!
We bore the bluff many-wived king, rough rival and victor of Rome;
We bore the stern despot-protector, whose dawning and sunset were gloom;
For they temper'd the self of the tyrant with love of the land,

Loyal to England;—the heart refraining the clutch of the hand.
But John's was blackness of darkness, a day of vileness and shame;
Shrieks of the tortured, and silence, and outrage the mouth cannot name.
—O that cry of the helpless, the weak that writhe under the foe,
Wrong man-wrought upon man, dumb unwritten annals of woe!
Cry that goes upward from earth as she rolls through the peace of the skies
'How long? Hast thou forgotten, O God!' . . and silence replies!
Silence :—and then was the answer;—the light o'er Windsor that broke,
The Meadow of Law—true Avalon where the true Arthur awoke!
—Not thou, whose name, as a seed o'er the world, plume-wafted on air,
Britons on each side sea,—Caerleon and Cumbria,—share,
Joy of a downtrod race, dear hope of freedom to-be,
Dream of poetic hearts, whom the vision only can see! . . .
For thine were the fairy knights, fair ideals of beauty and song;

But ours, in the ways of men, walk'd sober, and stumbling, and strong;—
Stumbling as who in peril and twilight their pathway trace out,
Hard to trace, and untried, and the foe above and about;
For the Charter of Freedom, the voice of the land in her Council secure
All doing, all daring,—and, e'en when defeated, of victory sure!
Langton, our Galahad, first, stamp'd Leader by Rome unaware,
Pembroke and Mowbray, Fitzwarine, Fitzalan, Fitzwalter, De Clare :—
—O fair temple of Freedom and Law!—the foundations ye laid :—
But again came the storm, and the might of darkness and wrong was array'd,
A warfare of years; and the battle raged, and new heroes arose
From a soil that is fertile in manhood's men, and scatter'd the foes,
And set in their place the bright pillars of Order, Liberty's shrine,
O'er the land far-seen, as o'er Athens the home of Athena divine.

—So the land had rest :—and the cloud of that heart-sore struggle and pain
Rose from her ancient hills, and peace shone o'er her again;
Sunlike chasing the 'plagues wherewith the land was defiled;
And the leprosy fled, and her flesh came again, as the flesh of a child.
For now the great Law-giver comes, Justinian himself of his realm,
Edward, since Alfred our greatest of all who have watch'd by the helm!
He who yet preaches in silence his life-word, the light of his way,
From his marble unadorn'd chest, in the heart of the West Minster gray,
Keep thy Faith . . . In the great town-twilight, this city of gloom,
—O how unlike that blithe London he look'd on !—I look on his tomb,
In the circle of kings, round the shrine, where the air is heavy with fame,
Dust of our moulder'd chieftains, and splendour shrunk to a name.
Silent synod august, ye that tried the delight and the pain,
Trials and snares of a throne, was the legend written in vain?

Speak, for ye know, crown'd shadows! who down each narrow and strait
As ye might, once guided,—a perilous passage,—the keel of the State,
Fourth Henry, fourth Edward, Elizabeth, Charles,—now ye rest from your toil,
Was it best, when by truth and compass ye steer'd, or by statecraft and guile?
Or is it so hard, that steering of States, that as men who throw in
With party their life, honour soils his own ermine, a lie is no sin? . . .
—Not so, great Edward, with thee,—not so!—For he learn'd in his youth
The step straightforward and sure, the proud, bright bearing of truth:—
Arm'd against Simon at Evesham, yet not less, striking for Law,—
Ages of temperate freedom, a vision of order, he saw!—
—Vision of opulent years, a murmur of welfare and peace:
Orchard golden-globed, plain waving in golden increase;
Hopfields fairer than vineyards, green laughing tendrils and bine;
Woodland misty in sunlight, and meadow sunny with kine;—

Havens of heaving blue, where the keels of Guienne and the Hanse
Jostle and creak by the quay, and the mast goes up like a lance,
Gay with the pennons of peace, and, blazon'd with Adria's dyes,
Purple and orange, the sails like a sunset burn in the skies.
Bloodless conquests of commerce, that nation with nation unite!
Hand clasp'd frankly in hand, not steel-clad buffets in fight!
On the deck strange accents and shouting; rough fur-cowl'd men of the north,
Genoa's brown-neck'd sons, and whom swarthy Smyrna sends forth:
Freights of the south; drugs potent o'er death from the basilisk won,
Odorous Phoenix-nest, and spice of a sunnier sun:—
Butts of Malvasian nectar, Messene's vintage of old,
Cyprian webs, damask of Arabia mazy with gold:
Sendal and Samite and Tarsien, and sardstones ruddy as wine,
Graved by Athenian diamond with forms of beauty divine.
To the quay from the gabled alleys, the huddled ravines of the town,

Twilights of jutting fretwork and oak, the Guild-merchants come down,
Cheapening the gifts of the south, the sea-borne alien bales,
For the snow-bright fleeces of Leom'ster, the wealth of Devonian vales;
While above them, the cavernous gates, on which knight-robbers have gazed
Hopeless, in peace look down, their harrows of iron upraised;
And Dustyfoot enters at will with his gay Autolycus load,
And the maidens are flocking as doves when they fling the light grain on the road.
Low on the riverain mead, where the dull clay-cottages cling
To the tall town-ward and the towers, as nests of the martin in spring,
Where the year-long fever lurks, and gray leprosy burrows secure,
Are the wattled huts of the Friars, the long, white Church of the poor:
—Haven of wearied eyelids; of hearts that care not to live;
Shadow and silence of prayer; the peace which the world cannot give!

Tapers hazily gleaming through fragrance the censers outpour;
Chant ever rising and rippling in sweetness, as waves on the shore;
Casements of woven stone, with more than the rainbow bedyed;
Beauty of holiness! Spell yet unbroken by riches and pride!
—Ah! could it be so for ever!—the good aye better'd by Time;—
First-Faith, first-Wisdom, first-Love,—to the end be true to their prime! . . .
Far rises the storm o'er horizons unseen, that will lay them in dust,
Crashings of plunder'd cloisters, and royal insatiate lust:—
Far, unseen, unheard!—Meanwhile the great Minster on high
Like a stream of music, aspiring, harmonious, springs to the sky:—
Story on story ascending their buttress'd fretwork unfold,
Till the highest height is attain'd, and the Cross shines starlike in gold,
Set as a meteor in heaven; a sign of health and release:—
And the land rejoices below, and the heart-song of England is Peace.

THE REJOICING OF THE LAND 73

This date has been chosen as representing at once the culminating point in the reign of Edward, and of Mediaevalism in England. The sound, the fascinating elements of that period rapidly decline after the thirteenth century in Church and State, in art and in learning.

'In the person of the great Edward,' says Freeman, 'the work ' of reconciliation is completed. Norman and Englishman have ' become one under the best and greatest of our later Kings, the ' first who, since the Norman entered our land, . . . followed a ' purely English policy.'

The three children: William I and II, and Henry I.

The transept: of Canterbury Cathedral, after Becket's death named the 'Martyrdom.'

Nor again: See the *Early Plantagenets*, by Stubbs: one of the very few masterpieces among the shoal of little books on great subjects in which a declining age is fertile.

Britons on each side sea: Armorica and Cornwall, Wales and Strathclyde, all share in the great Arthurian legend.

Justinian: 'Edward,' says Stubbs, 'is the great lawgiver, the ' great politician, the great organiser of the mediaeval English ' polity': (*Early Plantagenets*).

Keep thy Faith: 'Pactum serva' may be still seen inscribed on the huge stone coffin of Edward I.

The keels of Guienne . . . Adria's dyes: The ships of Gascony, of the Hanse Towns, of Genoa, of Venice, are enumerated amongst those which now traded with England.

Malvasian nectar: 'Malvoisie,' the sweet wine of the Southern Morea, gained its name from Monemvasia, or Napoli di Malvasia, its port of shipment.

Sendal: A thin rich silk. *Tarsien:* Silken stuff from Tartary. *Samite:* A very rich stuff, sometimes wholly of silk, often crimson, interwoven with gold and silver thread, and embroidered.

Athenian diamond: A few very fine early gems ascribed to Athens, are executed wholly with diamond-point.

The snow-bright fleeces: Those of Leominster were very long famous.

Devonian vales: The ancient mining region west of Tavistock.

Dustyfoot: Old name for pedlar.

CRECY

August 26 : 1346

At Creçy by Somme in Ponthieu
   High up on a windy hill
A mill stands out like a tower;
   King Edward stands on the mill.
The plain is seething below
   As Vesuvius seethes with flame,
But O! not with fire, but gore,
Earth incarnadined o'er,
   Crimson with shame and with fame :—
To the King run the messengers, crying
'Thy Son is hard-press'd to the dying!'
  —'Let alone: for to-day will be written in story
   'To the great world's end, and for ever:
    'So let the boy have the glory.'

   Erin and Gwalia there
    With England are rank'd against France;
   Outfacing the oriflamme red
    The red dragons of Merlin advance :—

As a harvest in autumn renew'd
    The lances bend o'er the fields;
Snow-thick our arrow-heads white
Level the foe as they light;
    Knighthood to yeomanry yields :—
Proud heart, the King watches, as higher
Goes the blaze of the battle, and nigher :—
  'To-day is a day will be written in story
    'To the great world's end, and for ever!
      'Let the boy alone have the glory.'

Harold at Senlac-on-Sea
    By Norman arrow laid low,—
When the shield-wall was breach'd by the shaft,
    —Thou art avenged by the bow!
Chivalry! name of romance!
    Thou art henceforth but a name!
Weapon that none can withstand,
Yew in the Englishman's hand,
    Flight-shaft unerring in aim!
As a lightning-struck forest the foemen
Shiver down to the stroke of the bowmen :—
  —'O to-day is a day will be written in story
    'To the great world's end, and for ever!
      'So, let the boy have the glory.'

Pride of Liguria's shore
  Genoa wrestles in vain;
Vainly Bohemia's King
  Kinglike is laid with the slain.
The Blood-lake is wiped out in blood,
  The shame of the centuries o'er;
Where the pride of the Norman had sway
The lions lord over the fray,
  The legions of France are no more :—
—The Prince to his father kneels lowly;
—' His is the battle! his wholly!
  ' For to-day is a day will be written in story
    ' To the great world's end, and for ever :—
      ' So, let him have the spurs, and the glory!'

Erin and Gwalia; Half of Edward's army consisted of light-armed footmen from Ireland and Wales—the latter under their old Dragon-flag.

Chivalry : The feudal idea of an army, resting ' on the superiority ' of the horseman to the footman, of the mounted noble to the ' unmounted churl,' may be said to have been ruined by this battle ': (*Green*, B. IV : ch. iii).

Liguria : 15,000 cross-bowmen from Genoa were in Philip's army.

The Blood-lake : Senlac.

THE BLACK DEATH

1348-9

BLUE and ever more blue
The sky of that summer's spring:
No cloud from dawning to night:
The lidless eyeball of light
Glared: nor could e'en in darkness the dew
　　Her pearls on the meadow-grass string.
　　As a face of a hundred years,
　　Mummied and scarr'd, for the heart
　　Is long dry at the fountain of tears,
　　Green earth lay brown-faced and torn,
　　Scarr'd and hard and forlorn.
　　And as that foul monster of Lerna
　　Whom Héraclés slew in his might,
　　But this one slaying, not slain,
　　From the marshes, poisonous, white,
Crawl'd out a plague-mist and sheeted the plain,
　　A hydra of hell and night.
—Whence upon men has that horror past?

From Cathaya westward it stole to Byzance,—
The City of Flowers,—the cities of France ;—
O'er the salt-sea ramparts of England, last,
Reeking and rank, a serpent's breath :—
What is this, men cry in their fear, what is this that cometh?
'Tis the Black Death, they whisper :
The black black Death!

The heart of man at the name
To a ball of ice shrinks in,
With hope, surrendering life :—
The husband looks on the wife,
Reading the tokens of doom in the frame,
The pest-boil hid in the skin,
And flees and leaves her to die.
Fear-sick, the mother beholds
In her child's pure crystalline eye
A dull shining, a sign of despair.
Lo, the heavens are poison, not air ;
And they fall as when lambs in the pasture
With a moan that is hardly a moan,
Drop, whole flocks, where they stand ;
And the mother lays her, alone,
Slain by the touch of her nursing hand,
Where the household before her is strown.

—Earth, Earth, open and cover thy dead !
For they are smitten and fall who bear
The corpse to the grave with a prayerless prayer,
While thousands are crush'd in the common bed :—
—Is it Hell that breathes with an adder's breath ?
Is it the day of doom, men cry, the Judge that cometh ?
—'Tis the Black Death, God help us !
The black black Death.

Maid Alice and maid Margaret
In the fields have built them a bower
Of reedmace and rushes fine,
Fenced with sharp albespyne ;
Pretty maids hid in the nest; and yet
Yours is one death, and one hour !
Priest and peasant and lord
By the swift, soft stroke of the air,
By a silent invisible sword,
In plough-field or banquet, fall :
The watchers are flat on the wall :—
Through city and village and valley
The sweet-voiced herald of prayer
Is dumb in the towers ; the throng
To the shrine pace barefoot ; and where
Blazed out from the choir a glory of song,
God's altar is lightless and bare.

Is there no pity in earth or sky?
The burden of England, who shall say?
Half the giant oak is riven away,
And the green leaves yearn for the leaves that die.
Will the whole world drink of the dragon's breath?
It is the cup, men cry, the cup of God's fury that cometh!
    'Tis the Black Death, God help us;
      The black black Death.

    In England is heard a moan,
    A bitter lament and a sore,
    Rachel lamenting her dead,
    And will not be comforted
For the little faces for ever gone,
    · The feet from the silent floor.
    And a cry goes up from the land,
    Take from us in mercy, O God,
    Take from us the weight of thy hand,
    The cup and the wormwood of woe!
    'Neath the terrible barbs of thy bow
    This England, this once thy beloved,
    Is water'd with life-blood for rain;
    The bones of her children are white,
    As flints on the Golgotha plain;
Not slain as warriors by warriors in fight,
    By the arrows of Heaven slain.

We have sinn'd : we lift up our souls to thee,
O Lord God eternal on high :
Thou who gavest thyself to die,
Saviour, save ! to thy feet we flee :—
Snatch from the hell and the Enemy's breath,
From the Prince of the Air, from the terror by night that
    cometh :—
From the Black Death, Christ save us !
The black black Death !

From the Marshes : The drought which preceded the plague in England, and may have predisposed to its reception, was followed by mist, in which the people fancied they saw the disease palpably advancing.

From Cathaya : The plague was heard of in Central Asia in 1333 ; it reached Constantinople in 1347.

The City of Flowers : Florence, where the ravages of the plague were immortalized by the *Decamerone* of Boccaccio.

The pest-boil : Seems to have been the enlarged and discharging gland by which the specific blood-poison of the plague relieved itself. A 'muddy glistening' of the eye is noticed as one of the symptoms.

The common bed : More than 50,000 are said to have been buried on the site of the Charter House.

Albespyne : Hawthorn.

Half the giant oak : 'Of the three or four millions who then 'formed the population of England, more than one-half were swept 'away': (*Green*, B. IV : ch. iii).

THE PILGRIM AND THE PLOUGHMAN

1382

It is a dream, I know :—Yet on the past
Of this dear England if in thought we gaze,
About her seems a constant sunshine cast;
In summer calm we see and golden haze
The little London of Plantagenet days;
Quaint labyrinthine knot of toppling lanes,
And thorny spires aflame with starlike vanes.

Our silver Thames all yet unspoil'd and clear;
The many-buttress'd bridge that stems the tide;
Black-timber'd wharves; arcaded walls, that rear
Long, golden-crested roofs of civic pride :—
While flaunting galliots by the gardens glide,
And on Spring's frolic air the May-song swells,
Mix'd with the music of a thousand bells.

Beyond the bridge a mazy forest swims,
Great spars and sails and flame-tongued flags on high,
Wedged round the quay, a-throng with ruddy limbs
And faces bronzed beneath another sky:
And 'mid the press sits one with aspect shy
And downcast eyes of watching, and, the while,
The deep observance of an inward smile.

In hooded mantle gray he smiled and sate,
With ink-horn at his knees and scroll and pen,
And took the toll and register'd the freight,
'Mid noise of clattering cranes and strife of men:
And all that moved and spoke was in his ken,
In hues and lines like Nature's own design'd
Within the magic mirror of his mind.

Thence oft, returning homeward, on the book,—
His of Certaldo, or the bard whose lays
Were lost to love in Scythia,—he would look
Till his fix'd eyes the dancing letters daze:
Then forth to the near fields, and feed his gaze
On one fair flower in starry myriads spread,
And in her graciousness be comforted :—

Then, joyous with a poet's joy, to draw
With genial touch, and strokes of patient skill,
The very image of each thing he saw:—
He limn'd the man all round, for good or ill,
Having both sighs and laughter at his will;
And picture-like his soul the world survey'd,
Yet stood outside the picture that he made.

—Man's inner passions in their conscience-strife,
The conflicts of the heart against the heart,
The mother yearning o'er the infant's life,
The maiden wrong'd by wealth and lecherous art,
The leper's loathsome cell from man apart,
War's savage lust and fire, the village-woe,
The tinsel chivalry veiling shame below,—

Not his to draw,—to see, perhaps :—Our eyes
Hold bias with our humour :—His, to paint
With Nature's freshness, what before him lies:
The knave, the fool; the frolicsome, the quaint:
His the broad jest, the laugh without restraint,
The ready tears, the spirit lightly moved;
Loving the world, and by the world beloved.

So forth fared Chaucer on his pilgrimage
Through England's humours; in immortal song
Bodying the form and pressure of his age,
Tints gay as pure, and delicate as strong;
Still to the Tabard the blythe travellers throng,
Seen in his mind so vividly, that we
Know them more clearly than the men we see.

Fair France, bright Italy those numbers train'd;
First in his pages Nature wedding Art
Of all our sons of song; yet he remain'd
True English of the English at his heart:—
He stood between two worlds, yet had no part
In that new order of the dawning day
Which swept his realm of chivalry away.

O Poet of romance and courtly glee
And downcast eager glance that shuns the sky,
Above, about, are signs thou canst not see;
Portents in heaven and earth!—And one goes by
With other than thy prosperous, laughing eye,
Framing the rough web of his rueful lays,
The sorrow and the sin;—with bitter gaze

As down the Strand he stalks, a sable shade
Of death, while, jingling like the elfin train,
In silver samite knight and dame and maid
Ride to the tourney on the barrier'd plain;
And he must bow in humble mute disdain,
And that worst woe of baffled souls endure,
To see the evil that they may not cure.

For on sweet Malvern Hill one morn he lay,
Drowsed by the music of the constant stream :—
Loud sang the cuckoo, cuckoo !—for the May
Breathed summer : summer floating like a dream
From the far fields of childhood, with a gleam
Of alien freshness on her forehead fair,
And Heaven itself within the common air.

Then on the mead in vision Langland saw
A pilgrim-throng; not missal-bright as those
Whom Chaucer's hand surpass'd itself to draw,
Gay as the lark, and brilliant as the rose ;—
But such as dungeon foul or spital shows,
Or the serf's fever-den, or field of fight,
When festering sunbeams on the wounded smite.

No sainted shrine the motley wanderers seek,
Pilgrims of life upon the field of scorn,
Mocking and mock'd; with plague and hunger weak,
And haggard faces bleach'd as those who mourn,
And footsteps redden'd with the trodden thorn;
Blind stretching hands that grope for truth in vain,
Across a twilight meteor-haunted plain.

A land whose children toil and rot like beasts,
Robbers and robb'd by turns, the dreamer sees:—
Land of poor-grinding lords and faithless priests,
Where wisdom starves and folly thrones at ease
'Mid lavishness and lusts and knaveries;
Times out of joint, a universe of lies,
Till Love divine appear in Ploughman's guise

To burn the gilded tares and save the land,
Risen from the grave and walking earth again:—
—And as he dream'd and kiss'd the nail-pierced hand,
A hundred towers their Easter voices rain
In silver showers o'er hill and vale and plain,
And the air throbb'd with sweetness, and he woke;
And all the dream in light and music broke.

—He look'd around, and saw the world he left
When to that visionary realm of song
His spirit fled from bonds of flesh bereft;
And on the vision he lay musing long,
As o'er his soul rude minstrel-echoes throng,
Old measures half-disused; and grasp'd his pen,
And drew his cottage-Christ for homely men.

Thus Langland also took his pilgrimage;
Rough lone knight-errant on uncourtly ways,
And wrong and woe were charter'd on his page,
With some horizon-glimpse of sweeter days.
And on the land the message of his lays
Smote like the strong North-wind, and cleansed the sky
With wholesome blast and bitter clarion-cry,

Summoning the people in the Ploughman's name.
—So fought his fight, and pass'd unknown away;
Seeking no other praise, no sculptured fame,
Nor laureate honours for his artless lay,
Nor in the Minster laid with high array;—
But where the May-thorn gleams, the grasses wave,
And the wind sighs o'er a forgotten grave.

THE PILGRIM AND THE PLOUGHMAN   89

Langland, whom I have put here in contrast with Chaucer, is said to have lived between 1332 and 1400. His *Vision of Piers the Plowman*, with some added poems, forms an allegory on life in England, in Church and State, as it appeared to him during the dislocated and corrupt age which followed the superficial glories of Edward the Third's earlier years.

Took the toll: Amongst other official employments, Chaucer was Comptroller of the Customs in the Port of London. See his *House of Fame;* and the beautiful picture of his walks at dawning in the daisy-meadows: Prologue to the *Legend of Good Women*.

His of Certaldo, . . . *in Scythia:* Boccaccio:—and Ovid, who died in exile at Tomi, to both of whom Chaucer is greatly indebted for the substance of his tales.

Picture-like: 'It is chiefly as a comic poet, and a minute ob-
' server of manners and circumstances, that Chaucer excels. In
' serious and moral poetry he is frequently languid and diffuse, but
' he springs like Antaeus from the earth when his subject changes
' to coarse satire or merry narrative' (Hallam, *Mid. Ag.* Ch. IX: Pt. iii).

The Tabard: Inn in Southwark whence the pilgrims to Canterbury start.

Down the Strand: It is thus that Langland describes himself and his feelings of dissatisfaction with the world.

That worst woe: Literature, even ancient literature, has no phrase more deeply felt and pathetic than the words which the Persian nobleman at the feast in Thebes before Plataea addressed to Thersander of Orchomenus:—'Εχθίστη ὀδύνη τῶν ἐν ἀνθρώποισι, πολλὰ φρονέοντα μηδενὸς κρατέειν: (*Herodotus*, IX: xvi).

One morn he lay: The *Vision* opens with a picture of the poet asleep on Malvern Hill: the last of the added poems closing as he wakes with the Easter chimes.

Old measures: Langland's metre 'is more uncouth than that of
' his predecessors' (Hallam, *Mid. Ag.* Ch. IX: Pt. iii).

On the land: 'Langland's poem,' says S. Brooke, 'wrought so
' strongly in men's minds that its influence was almost as widely
' spread as Wiclif's in the revolt which had now begun against
' Latin Christianity': (*Primer of English Literature*, Ch. II).

In the Minster: Chaucer was buried at the entrance of St. Benet's Chapel in Westminster Abbey.

JEANNE D'ARC

1424

So many stars in heaven,—
Flowers in the meadow that shine;
—This little one of Domremy,
What special grace is thine?
By the fairy beech and the fountain
What but a child with thy brothers?
Among the maids of the valley
Art more than one among others?

Chosen darling of Heaven,
Yet at heart wast only a child!
And for thee the wild things of Nature
Set aside their nature wild:—
The brown-eyed fawn of the forest
Came silently glancing upon thee;
The squirrel slipp'd down from the fir,
And nestled his gentleness on thee.

Angelus bell and *Ave*,
Like voices they follow the maid
As she follows her sheep in the valley
From the dawn to the folding shade :—
For the world that we cannot see
Is the world of her earthly seeing;
From the air of the hills of God
She draws her breath and her being.

Dances by beech tree and fountain,
They know her no longer :—apart
Sitting with thought and with vision
In the silent shrine of the heart.
And a voice henceforth and for ever
Within, without her, is sighing
' Pity for France, O pity,
' France the beloved, the dying ! '

And now between church-wall and cottage
Who comes in the blinding light,
—Rainbow plumes and armour,
Face as the sun in his height. . . .
' Angel that pierced the red dragon,
' Pity for France, O pity !
' Holy one, thou shalt save her,
' Vineyard and village and city ! '

Poor sweet child of Domremy,
In thine innocence only strong,
Thou seest not the treason before thee,
The gibe and the curse of the throng,—
The furnace-pile in the market
That licks out its flames to take thee;—
For He who loves thee in heaven
On earth will not forsake thee!

Poor sweet maid of Domremy,
In thine innocence secure,
Heed not what men say of thee,
The buffoon and his jest impure!
Nor care if thy name, young martyr,
Be the star of thy country's story:—
Mid the white-robed host of the heavens
Thou hast more than glory!

Angel that pierced: 'She *had pity,* to use the phrase for ever on
'her lip, *on the fair realm of France.* She saw visions; St. Michael
'appeared to her in a flood of blinding light': (*Green*, B. IV: ch. vi).

TOWTON FIELD

Palm Sunday : 1461

LOVE, who from the throne above
Cam'st to teach the law of love,
Who thy peaceful triumph hast
Led o'er palms before thee cast,
E'en in highest heaven thine eyes
Turn from this day's sacrifice !
Slaughter whence no victor host
Can the palms of triumph boast ;
Blood on blood in rivers spilt,—
English blood by English guilt !

    From the gracious Minster-towers
    Of York the monks behold afar
The field of Towton shimmer like a star
With light of lance and helm ; while both the powers
Misnamed from the fair rose, with one fell blow,
    —In snow-dazed, blinding air
    Mass'd on the burnside bare,—
Each army, as one man, drove at the opposing foe.

Ne'er since then, and ne'er before,
On England's fields with English hands
Have met for death such myriad myriad bands,
Such wolf-like fury, and such greed of gore :—
No natural kindly touch, no check of shame :
And no such bestial rage
Blots our long story's page ;
Such lewd remorseless swords, such selfishness of aim.

—Gracious Prince of Peace ! Yet Thou
May'st look and bless with lenient eyes
When trodden races 'gainst their tyrant rise,
And the bent back no more will deign to bow :
Or when they crush some old anarchic feud,
And found the throne anew
On Law to Freedom true,
Cleansing the land they love from guilt of blood by blood.

Nor did Heaven unmoved behold
When Hellas, for her birthright free
Dappling with gore the dark Saronian sea,
The Persian wave back, past Abydos, roll'd :—
But in this murderous match of chief 'gainst chief
No chivalry had part,
No impulse of the heart ;
Nor any sigh for Right triumphant breathes relief.

  —Midday comes: and no release,
  No carnage-pause to blow on blow!
While through the choir the palm-wreathed children go,
And bright hosannas hail the Prince of Peace :—
And evening falls, and from the Minster height
   They see the wan Ouse stream
   Blood-dark with slaughter gleam,
And hear the demon-struggle shrieking through the night.

  Love, o'er palms in triumph strown
  Passing, through the crowd alone,—
  Silent 'mid the exulting cry,—
  At Jerusalem to die:
  Thou, foreknowing all, didst know
  How thy blood in vain would flow!
  How our madness oft would prove
  Recreant to the law of love:
  Wrongs that men from men endure
  Doing thee to death once more!

 'On the 29th of March 1461 the two armies encountered one
'another at Towton Field, near Tadcaster. In the numbers en-
'gaged, as well as in the terrible obstinacy of the struggle, no such
'battle had been seen in England since the field of Senlac. The
'two armies together numbered nearly 120,000 men': (*Green*,
B. IV : ch. vi).

 Saronian sea : Scene of the battle of Salamis, B.C. 480.

GROCYN AT OXFORD:

The English Renaissance.

1491

As she who in some village-child unknown,
With rustic grace and fantasy bedeck'd,
And in her simple loveliness alone,
A sister finds;—and the long years' neglect
Effaces with warm love and nursing care,
      And takes her heart to heart,
And in her treasured treasures bids her freely share,

    And robes with radiance new, new strength and
          grace:—
Hellas and England! thus it was with ye!
Though distanced far by centuries and by space,
Sisters in soul by Nature's own decree.
And if on Athens in her glory-day
      The younger might not look,
Her living soul came back, and reinfused our clay.

—It was not wholly lost, that better light,
Not in the darkest darkness of our day;
From cell to cell, e'en through the Danish night,
The torch ran on its firefly fitful way;
And blazed anew with him who in the vale
    Of fair Aosta saw
The careless reaper-bands, and pass'd the heavens' high
    pale,

And supp'd with God, in vision! Or with him,
Earliest and greatest of his name, who gave
His life to Nature, in her caverns dim
Tracking her soul, through poverty to the grave,
And left his Great Work to the barbarous age
    That, in its folly-love,
With wizard-fame defamed his and sweet Vergil's page.

But systems have their day, and die, or change
Transform'd to new: Not now from cloister cell
And desk-bow'd priest, breathes out that impulse
    strange
'Neath which the world of feudal Europe fell :—
Throes of new birth, new life; while men despair'd
    Or triumph'd in their pride,
As in their eyes the torch of learning fiercely flared.

For now the cry of Homer's clarion first
And Plato's golden tongue on English ears
And souls aflame for that new doctrine burst,
As Grocyn taught, when, after studious years,
He came from Arno to the liberal walls
    That welcomed me in youth,
And nursed in Grecian lore, long native to her halls.

O voice that spann'd the gulf of vanish'd years,
Evoking shapes of old from night to light,
Lo at thy spell a long-lost world appears,
Where Rome and Hellas open on their sight :—
The Gothic gloom disparts; a glory burns
    Behind the clouds of Time,
And all that wonder-past in beauty's strength returns.

—For when the Northern floods that lash'd and
    curl'd
Around the granite fragments of great Rome
Outspread Colossus-like athwart the world,
Foam'd down, and the new nations found their home,
That earlier Europe, law and arts and arms,
    Fell into far-off shade,
Or lay like some fair maid sleep-sunk in magic charms.

And as in lands once flourishing, now forlorn,
And desolate capitals, the traveller sees
Wild tribes, in ruins from the ruins torn
Hutted like beasts 'mid marble palaces,
Unknowing what those relics mean, and whose
  The goblets gold-enchased
And images of the gods the broken vaults disclose;

So in the Mid-age from the Past of Man
The Present was disparted; and they stood
As on some island, sever'd from the plan
Of the great world, and the sea's twilight flood
Around them, and the monsters of the unknown;
  Blind fancy mix'd with fact;
Faith in the things unseen sustaining them alone.

Age of extremes and contrasts !—where the good
Was more than human in its tenderness
Of chivalry;—beauty side by side with blood,
And evil raging with a wild excess
Of more than brutal :—A disjointed time !
  Doubt with Hypocrisy pair'd,
And purest Faith by folly, childlike, led to crime.

O Florentine, O Master, who alone
From thy loved Vergil till our Shakespeare came
Didst climb the long steps to the imperial throne,
With what immortal dyes of angry flame
Hast blazon'd out the vileness of the day!
    What tints of perfect love
Rosier than summer rose, etherealize thy lay!

—Now, as in some new land when night is deep
The pilgrim halts, nor knows what round him lies,
And wakes with dawn, and finds him on the steep,
While plains beneath and unguess'd summits rise,
And stately rivers streaming to the sea,
    Cities of men and towers,
Abash'd for very joy, and gazing fearfully;—

New worlds, new wisdom, a new birth of things
On Europe dawn, and men know where they stand:
The sea his western portal open flings,
And bold Sebastian strikes the flowery land:
Soon, heaven its secret yields; the golden sun
    Enthrones him in the midst,
And round his throne man and the planets humbly run.

New learning all! yet fresh from fountains old,
Hellenic inspiration, pure and deep:
Strange treasures of Byzantine hoards unroll'd,
And mouldering volumes from monastic sleep,
Reclad with life by more than magic art:
    Till that old world renew'd
His youth, and in the past the present had its part.

O vision that ye saw, and hardly saw,
Ye who in Alfred's path at Oxford trod,
Or in our London train'd by studious law
The little-ones of Christ to him and God,
Colet and Grocyn!—Though the world forget
    The labours of your love,
In loving hearts your names live in their fragrance yet.

O vision that our happier eyes have seen!
For not till peace came with Elizabeth
Did those fair maids of holy Hippocrene
Cross the wan seas and draw a northern breath:
Though Chaucer catching from Italian lyres
    Your far-off echoes, sang
Like her who sings ere dawn has lit his Eastern fires;—

Herald of that first splendour, when the sky
Was topaz-clear with hope, and life-blood-red
With thoughts of mighty poets, lavishly
Round all the fifty years' horizon shed :—
Now in our glades the Aglaian Graces gleam,
    Around our fountains throng,
And change Ilissus' banks for Thames and Avon stream.

Daughters of Zeus and bright Eurynomé,
She whose blue waters pave the Aegaean plain,
Children of all surrounding sky and sea,
A larger ocean claims you, not in vain !
Ye who to Helicon from Thessalia wide
    Wander'd when earth was young,
Come from Libethrion, come; our love, our joy, our pride!

Ah ! since your gray Pierian ilex-groves
Felt the despoiling tread of barbarous feet,
This land, o'er all, the Delian leader loves ;
Here is your favourite home, your genuine seat :—
In these green western isles renew the throne
    Where Grace by Wisdom shines ;
—We greet you with full hearts, and claim you for our own !

If, looking at England, one point may be singled out in that long movement, generalized under the name of the Renaissance, as critical, it is the introduction of Greek literature :—which has remained ever since conspicuously the most powerful and enlarging element, the most effectively educational, among all branches of human study.

In the vale Of fair Aosta : See Anselm's youthful vision of the gleaners and the palace of heaven (Green : *History*, B. II : ch. ii).

His Great Work: Roger Bacon's so-named *Opus Majus :* 'At ' once,' says Whewell, ' the Encyclopaedia and the Novum Organum ' of the thirteenth century.' Like Vergil, Bacon passed at one time for a magician.

That new doctrine : Grocyn was perhaps the first Englishman who studied Greek under Chalcondylas the Byzantine at Florence ; certainly the first who lectured on Greek in England. This was in the Hall of Exeter College, Oxford, in 1491. To him Erasmus (1499) came to study the language. See the brilliant account of the revival of learning in Green, *Hist.* B. V : ch. ii.

Master, who alone : See the *Poet's Euthanasia.*

Sebastian : Cabot, who, in 1497, sailed from Bristol and reached Florida.

The golden sun : Refers to Copernicus ; whose solar system was, however, not published till 1543.

The little-ones : Colet, Dean of St. Paul's, founded the school in 1510. ' The bent of its founder's mind was shown by the image of ' the Child Jesus over the master's chair, with the words *Hear ye* ' *Him* graven beneath it' (*Green :* B. V : ch. iv).

Fifty years : Between 1570 and 1620 lies almost all the glorious production of our so-called Elizabethan period.

From Libethrion :—Nymphae, noster amor, Libethrides ! . . . Alas, how the least little fragment of Vergilian music puts to shame and silences our modern rhythms !

MARGARET TUDOR:

Prothalamion

1502

LOVE who art above us all,
Guard the treasure on her way,
Flower of England, fair and tall,
Maiden-wise and maiden-gay,
As her northward path she goes;
Daughter of the double rose.

Look with twofold grace on her
Who from twofold root has grown,
Flower of York and Lancaster,
Now to grace another throne,
Rose in Scotland's garden set,—
Britain's only Margaret.

Exile-child from childhood's bower,
Pledge and bond of Henry's faith,
James, take home our English flower,
Guard from touch of scorn and skaith;
Bearing, in her slender hands,
Palms of peace to hostile lands.

Safe by southern smiling shires,
Many a city, many a shrine;
By the newly kindled fires
Of the black Northumbrian mine;
Border clans in ambush set;
Carry thou fair Margaret.

—Land of heath and hill and linn,
Land of mountain-freedom wild,
She in heart to thee is kin,
Tudor's daughter, Gwynedd's child!
In her lively lifeblood share
Angharad and Gwenllian fair.

East and West, from Dee to Yare,
Now in equal bonds are wed:
Peace her new-found flower shall wear,
Rose that dapples white with red;
North and South, dissever'd yet,
Join in this fair Margaret!

Ocean round our Britain roll'd,
Sapphire ring without a flaw,
When wilt thou one realm enfold,
One in freedom, one in law?
Will that ancient feud be sped,
Brothers' blood by brothers shed?

—Land with freedom's struggle sore,
Land to whom thy children cling
With a lover's love and more,
Take the gentle gift we bring!
Pearl in thy crown-royal set;
Scotland's other Margaret.

Margaret Tudor, daughter to Henry VII, married in 1502 to James IV, and afterwards to Lord Angus, was thus great-grandmother on both sides to James I of England.

Gwynedd's child: The Tudors intermarried with the old royal family of North Wales, in whose pedigree occur the girl-names Gwenllian and Angharad.

Other Margaret: Sister to Edgar the Etheling, and wife to Malcolm. Her life and character are in contrast to the unhappy and unsatisfactory career of Margaret Tudor, whom I have here only treated as at once representing and uniting England, Scotland, and Wales.

LONDON BRIDGE

July 6 : 1535

THE midnight moaning stream
Draws down its glassy surface through the bridge
That o'er the current casts a tower'd ridge,
Dark sky-line forms fantastic as a dream ;
And cresset watch-lights on the bridge-gate gleam,
Where 'neath the star-lit dome gaunt masts upbuoy
No flag of festive joy,
But blanching spectral heads ;—their heads, who died
Victims to tyrant-pride,
Martyrs of Faith and Freedom in the day
Of shame and flame and brutal selfish sway.

And one in black array
Veiling her Rizpah-misery, to the gate
Comes, and with gold and moving speech sedate
Buys down the thing aloft, and bears away
Snatch'd from the withering wind and ravens' prey :

And as a mother's eyes, joy-soften'd, shed
Tears o'er her young child's head,
Golden and sweet, from evil saved; so she
O'er this, sad-smilingly,
Mangled and gray, unwarm'd by human breath,
Clasping death's relic with love passing death.

So clasping now! and so
When death clasps her in turn! e'en in the grave
Nursing the precious head she could not save,
Though through each drop her life-blood yearn'd to flow
If but for him she might to scaffold go :—
And O! as from that Hall, with innocent gore
Sacred from roof to floor,
To that grim other place of blood he went—
What cry of agony rent
The twilight,—cry as of an Angel's pain,—
My father, O my father! . . . and in vain!

Then, as on those who lie
Cast out from bliss, the days of joy come back,
And all the soul with wormwood sweetness rack,
So in that trance of dreadful ecstasy
The vision of her girlhood glinted by :—
And how the father through their garden stray'd,
And, child with children, play'd,

And teased the rabbit-hutch, and fed the dove
Before him from above
Alighting, in his visitation sweet,
Led on by little hands, and eager feet.

Hence among those he stands,
Elect ones, ever in whose ears the word
He that offends these little ones . . . is heard;
With love and kisses smiling-out commands,
And all the tender hearts within his hands;
Seeing, in every child that goes, a flower
From Eden's nursery bower,
A little stray from Heaven, for reverence here
Sent down, and comfort dear:
All care well paid-for by one pure caress,
And life made happy in their happiness.

He too, in deeper lore
Than woman's in those early days, or yet,
Train'd step by step his youthful Margaret;
The wonders of that amaranthine store
Which Hellas and Hesperia evermore
Lavish, to strengthen and refine the race:—
For, in his large embrace,
The light of faith with that new light combined
To purify the mind:—

A crystal soul, a heart without disguise,
All wisdom's lover, and through love, all-wise.

—O face she ne'er will see,—
Gray eyes, and careless hair, and mobile lips
From which the shaft of kindly satire slips
Healing its wound with human sympathy;
The heart-deep smile; the tear-concealing glee!
O well-known furrows of the reverend brow!
Familiar voice, that now
She will not hear nor answer any more,—
Till on the better shore
Where love completes the love in life begun,
And smoothes and knits our ravell'd skein in one.

Blest soul, who through life's course
Didst keep the young child's heart unstain'd and whole,
To find again the cradle at the goal,
Like some fair stream returning to its source;—
Ill fall'n on days of falsehood, greed, and force!
Base days, that win the plaudits of the base,
Writ to their own disgrace,
With casuist sneer o'erglossing works of blood,
Miscalling evil, good;
Before some despot-hero falsely named
Grovelling in shameful worship unashamed.

—But they of the great race
Look equably, not caring much, on foe
And fame and misesteem of man below;
And with forgiving radiance on their face,
And eyes that aim beyond the bourne of space,
Seeing the invisible, glory-clad, go up
And drink the absinthine cup,
Fill'd nectar-deep by the dear love of him
Slain at Jerusalem
To free them from a tyrant worse than this,
Changing brief anguish for the heart of bliss.

Envoy

—O moaning stream of Time,
Heavy with hate and sin and wrong and woe
As ocean-ward dost go,
Thou also hast thy treasures !—Life, sublime
In its own sweet simplicity :—life for love :
Heroic martyr-death :—
Man sees them not : but they are seen above.

One in black array : Sir T. More's daughter, Margaret Roper.
That Hall : Westminster, where More was tried : *That other place :* Tower Hill.
The vision of her childhood : More taught his own children, and was like a child with them. He ' would take grave scholars and

'statesmen into the garden to see his girls' rabbit-hutches. . . . *I have given you kisses enough*, he wrote to his little ones, *but stripes hardly ever*': (*Green*, B. V : ch. ii).

The wonders: See note to *Grocyn at Oxford*.

In his large embrace : More may be said to have represented the highest aim and effort of the 'new learning' in England. He is the flower of our Renaissance in genius, wisdom, and beauty of nature. 'Whenever,' says Erasmus in a famous passage, 'did Nature mould a character more gentle, endearing, and happy, than Thomas More's?'

A BALLAD OF QUEEN CATHARINE

January : 1536

WHY is it thus with me, false Love,
    Why is it thus with me?
Mine enemies might so have dealt;
    I fear'd it not of thee!

Thou wast the thought of all my thoughts,
    Nor other hope had I :
My life was laid upon thy love;
    Then how could'st let me die?

The flower is loyal to the bud,
    The greenwood to the spring,
The soldier to his banner bright,
    The noble to his king :

The bee is constant to the hive,
    The ringdove to the tree,
The martin to the cottage-eaves :
    Thou only not to me.

Ah! hapless fate of maiden hearts
    On others' alms to live,
And find their love with scorn flung out,
    Yet have but love to give!

The bud that in the better clime,
    Castilian sunshine, grew,
The stainless flower of love I brought,
    The rose of girlhood true,

To thee, O cruel king and cold,
    Cold as these icy skies!
—Ah shameful scorn of maiden shame
    And maiden sacrifice!

Ah baby face that came to glad
    Thy mother in her woes!
Now riven from thy mother's knee,
    And nursed amidst her foes!

—Yet oft the thorn-closed ways of life
    To love once green and dear,
As childhood passes to and fro,
    The little footsteps clear.

And if again thy father's feet
>   To tread the path should burn,
—O Love! e'en if for me too late,
>   Return, I cry, return!

And stand beside thy Catharine's bier,
>   And thou wilt surely see
That I have been as true to love
>   As thou wert false to me.

AT FOUNTAINS

1539

BLEST hour, as on green happy slopes I lie,
    Gray walls around and high,
While long-ranged arches lessen on the view,
    And one high gracious curve
Of shaftless window frames the limpid blue.

—God's altar erst, where wind-set rowan now
    Waves its green-finger'd bough,
And the brown tiny creeper mounts the bole
    With curious eye alert,
And beak that tries each insect-haunted hole,

And lives her gentle life from nest to nest,
    And dies undispossess'd:
Whilst all the air is quick with noise of birds
    Where once the chant went up;
Now musical with a song more sweet than words.

Sky-roof'd and bare and deep in dewy sod,
    Still 'tis the house of God!
Beauty by desolation unsubdued :—
    And all the past is here,
Thronging with thought this holy solitude.

I see the taper-stars, the altars gay;
    And those who crouch and pray;
The dun-robed crowd in close monastic stole,
    Who hither fled the world
To find the world again within the soul.

Yet here the pang of Love's defeat, the pride
    Of life unsatisfied,
Have found repose or anodyne; here the weak,
    Armour'd against themselves,
Might change true guiding for obedience meek.

Through day, through night, here, in the fragrant air,
    Their hours are struck by prayer;
Freed from the bonds of freedom, the distress
    Of choice, on life's storm-sea
They gaze unharm'd, and know their happiness.

Till o'er this rock of refuge, deem'd secure,
    —This palace of the poor,
Ascetic luxury, wealth too frankly shown,—
    The royal robber swept
His lustful eye, and seized the prey his own.

—O calm of Nature! Now thou hold'st again
    Thy sweet and silent reign!
And, as our feverish years their orbit roll,
    This gray and cloister'd peace
In its old healing virtue bathes the souL

1539 is the year when the greater monasteries, amongst which Fountains in Yorkshire held a prominent place, were dissolved and confiscated by Henry VIII.

The tiny creeper: Certhia Familiaris; the smallest of our birds after the wren. It belongs to a class nearly related to the woodpecker.

SIR HUGH WILLOUGHBY

1553-4

Two ships upon the steel-blue Arctic seas
When day was long and night itself was day,
Forged heavily before the South West breeze
As to the steadfast star they held their way;
Two specks of man, two only signs of life,
Where with all breathing things white Death keeps endless strife.

The Northern Cape is sunk: and to the crew
This zone of sea, with ice-floes wedged and rough,
Domed by its own pure height of tender blue,
Seems like a world from the great world cut off:
While, round the horizon clasp'd, a ring of white,
Snow-blink from snows unseen, walls them with angry light.

Now that long day compact of many days
Breaks up and wanes; and equal night beholds
Their hapless drifting past uncharted bays,
And in her chilling, killing arms enfolds:

While the near stars a thousand arrowy darts
Bend from their diamond eyes, as the low sun departs.

Or the weird Northern Dawn in idle play
Mocks their sad souls, now trickling down the sky
In many-quivering lines of golden spray,
Then blazing out, an Iris arch on high,
With fiery lances fill'd and feathery bars,
And sheeny veils that hide or half-reveal the stars.

A silent spectacle! Yet sounds, 'tis said,
On their forlornness broke; a hissing cry
Of mockery and wild laugh, as, overhead,
Those bright fantastic squadrons flaunted by:—
And that false dawn, long flickering, died away,
And the Sun came not forth, and Heaven withheld the day.

O King Hyperion, o'er the Delphic dale
Reigning meanwhile in glory, Ocean knew
Thine absence, and outstretch'd an icy veil,
A marble pavement, o'er his waters blue;
Past the Varangian fiord and Zembla hoar,
And from Petsora north to dark Arzina's shore:—

An iron ridge o'erhung with toppling snow
And giant beards of icicled cascade :—
Where, frost-imprison'd as the long months go,
The *Good Hope* and her mate-ship lay embay'd;
And those brave crews knew that all hope was gone;
England be seen no more; no more the living sun.

A store that daily lessens 'neath their eyes;
A little dole of light and fire and food :—
While Night upon them like a vampyre lies
Bleaching the frame and thinning out the blood;
And through the ships the frost-bit timbers groan,
And the Guloine prowls round, with dull heart-curdling moan.

Then sometimes on the soul, far off, how far!
Came back the shouting crowds, the cannon-roar,
The palace-windows glittering like a star,
The buoyant Thames, the green, sweet English shore,
The heartful prayers, the fireside blaze and bliss,
The little faces bright, and woman's last, last kiss.

—O yet, for all their misery, happy souls!
Happy in faith and love and fortitude;

In whom the thought of England dear controls
All shrinking of the flesh at death so rude;
Though long at rest in that far Arctic grave,
True sailor hero hearts, van of our bravest brave!

And one by one the North King's searching lance
Touch'd, and they stiffen'd at their task, and died;
And their stout leader glanced a farewell glance;
'God is as close by sea as land,' he cried,
'In his own light not nearer than this gloom,'—
And look'd as one who o'er the mountains sees his home.

Home!—happy sound of vanish'd happiness!
—But when the unwilling sun crept up again,
And loosed the sea from winter and duresse,
The seal-wrapt race that roams the Lapland main
Saw in Arzina, wondering, fearing more,
The tatter'd ships, in snows entomb'd and vaulted o'er:

And clomb the decks, and found the gallant crew,
As forms congeal'd to stone, where frozen fate
Took each man in his turn, and gently slew:—
Nor knew the heroic chieftain, as he sate,
English through every fibre, in his place,
The smile of duty done upon the steadfast face.

SIR HUGH WILLOUGHBY

Sir Hugh Willoughby, in the *Bona Esperanza*, with two other vessels, sailed 10th May 1553, saluting the palace of Greenwich as they passed. By September 18th he, with one consort, reached the harbour of Arzina, where all perished early in 1554. His will, dated January 1554, was found with the ships by Russians soon after.

Arzina is placed near the western headland of the White Sea, east of the Waranger Fiord, and west of Nova Zembla and the mouth of the Petchora.

LADY CATHERINE'S LAMENT

1562

O WARM soft arms, flung out once more
    To necklace me with love!
O captive caged in cruel walls,
    My dungeon-nestled dove!
His child, whom thou hast never seen,
    Sole sign of one so dear,
Whose eyes from thee look out on me,—
    Hush, lest the wicked hear!
I by thee and thou by me;—hush! thou art with thy
    mother:
Thou my only comfort art, baby! I have none other.

    Where is he, . . those dear searching eyes
        They ask, but ask in vain;
    They cannot pierce the dungeon stones,
        Nor solve the dungeon chain.
    O walls that hold my love and hide,
        Too near to be so far,

From this sad heart not less apart
   Than yonder evening star!

O cruel snares and trials set
   To torture loving hearts!
And cruel the revengeful pride
   That me from Edward parts:
As fiends that look on heaven, She hates
   Love's happy converse here,
And loads him with the chains of guilt,
   Because he is so dear.
O Queen! O Woman! does thy rage
   Jalouse me one caress?
Or canst thou ne'er the beauty share
   Of love's unselfishness?

Ah fount of love that springs so sweet
   And then so bitter turns!
Ah bliss of bygone days, that now
   My brain like madness burns!
O Love, to thee I cast my soul
   Forth on the space of sky,

And—thou with me, and I with thee!
Is all the heart can cry.

—O fold once more about my neck
Thy flower-soft embrace;
And once more press, and closer yet,
The little rosebud face;
And let me feel against my lips
The warmth of living breath,—
For murderous eyes and serpent spies
Are levell'd round for death:—
I by thee, and thou by me; hush!—thou art with thy mother:
Thou my only comfort art, baby!—I have none other.

Lady Catherine Grey, granddaughter to Mary Tudor, second sister to Henry VIII, after the death of her mother, Duchess of Suffolk, became heiress-presumptive to the throne under the will of Henry. On the discovery of her private marriage with Edward Seymour, Lord Hertford, 'the queen, always envious of the happi-
' ness of lovers, and jealous of all who could entertain any hopes
' of the succession' (Hallam: *Const. Hist.* ch. iii), imprisoned them both in separate dungeons within the Tower. The first child, (in whose son the dukedom of Somerset was restored by Charles II), was born 17th August 1561.

CROSSING SOLWAY

May 16 : 1568

Blow from the North, thou bitter North wind,
Blow over the western bay,
Where Nith and Eden and Esk run in
And fight with the salt sea spray,
And the sun shines high through the sailing sky
In the freshness of blue Mid-may.

Blow North-North-West, and hollow the sails
Of a Queen who slips over the sea
As a hare from the hounds; and her covert afar;
And now she can only flee;
And death before and the sisterly shore
That smiles perfidiously.

O Mid-may freshness about her cheek
And piercing her poor attire,
The rage of revenge thou canst not allay,
The fever of heart and the fire,
The death-despair for the days that were,
And famine of vain desire!

—On Holyrood stairs an iron-heel'd clank
Came up in the gloaming hour:
And iron fingers have bursten the bar
Of the palace innermost bower:
And fiend-like on her black Morton and Ker
And spectral Ruthven glower.

She hears the shriek as the Douglas horde
Hurry the victim beneath;
And she feels their dead man's grasp on her skirt
In the sudden horror of death;
And the dastard King at her bosom cling
With a serpent's poison-breath.

O fair girl Queen, well weep for the friend
To his faith too faithful and thee;
For a brother's hypocrite tears; for the flight
To the Castle set by the sea;
Where thy father's tomb lay open in gloom
'Twere better for thee to be!

O fair girl Queen! O better for thee
To lie under the rowan sod!
The tempters again are round thee, to tempt
Thy young feet the deathward road:
For man sins without shame when he dares to claim
The devil within him as God.

O too-too-woman, untimely born;
Frail flower of a treacherous time!
A friendless girl in a lawless land,
Seduced in beauty's prime,
By the men of blood, in thy passionate mood,
By crime to avenge thee on crime!

Ah desolate house by the Church in the field!
Secrets o'er-fearsome for sight! .
Thunder and flash like the terrors of God
When his lightnings the mountain-head smite:
Was she guilty? Who knows? for the craft of her foes
Stamps her with the shame of the night.

And the secret who knows of that fury-love
For the bold bad borderer Earl?
O Lord of the heart! was it thou breaking in,
A God over-match'd with a girl,
As the sea when he sweeps from his innermost deeps,
With a first, long, billowy swirl?

Was it thou, or that Anteros After-love,
Who mocks thine image too well,
Enchaining the woman to masterful man
By a shame-begotten spell,
That holds her forlorn by the wrong she has borne,
And frames a false heaven in hell?

—Fair Queen, who standest imploring the land
That lures thee to grief on grief,
White homes that smile o'er their orchard-slopes
And the bloom of the coming sheaf;
While the heart denies to the fever'd eyes
Their bitter-sweet relief:—

Turn aside, O Queen, from the cruel land,
From the greedy shore turn away;
From shame upon shame: But most shame for those
On their passionate captive who play
With a subtle net, hope alternate with threat,
Hung out to tempt her astray!

Poor scape-goat of crimes, where,—her part what it may,—
So tortured, so hunted to die,
Foul age of deceit and of hate,—on her head
Least stains of gore-guiltiness lie;
To the hearts of the just her blood from the dust
Not in vain for mercy will cry.

Poor scape-goat of nations and faiths in their strife
So cruel,—and thou so fair!
Poor girl!—so, best, in her misery named,—
Discrown'd of two kingdoms, and bare;
Not first nor last on this one was cast
The burden that others should share.

—When the race is convened at the great assize
And the last long trumpet-call,
If Woman 'gainst Man, in her just appeal,
At the feet of the Judge should fall,
O the cause were secure;—the sentence sure!
—But she will forgive him all!

O keen heart-hunger for days that were;
Last look at a vanishing shore!
In two short words all bitterness summ'd,
That *Has been* and *Nevermore!*
Nor with one caress will Mary bless,
Nor look on the babe she bore!

Blow, bitter wind, with a cry of death,
Blow over the western bay:
The sunshine is gone from the desolate girl,
And before is the doomster-day,
And the saw-dust red with the heart's-blood shed
In the shambles of Fotheringay.

Mary of Scotland is one of the five or six figures in our history who rouse an undying personal interest. Volumes have been and will be written on her:—yet if we put aside the distorting mists of national and political and theological partisanship, the common laws of human nature will give an easy clue to her conduct and that of her enemies.

Her flight from Scotland, as the turning-point in that unhappy and pathetic career, has been here chosen for the moment whence to survey it.

On Holyrood stairs: Rizzio was murdered on 9th March 1566. Mary's exclamation when she heard of his death next day, *No more tears ; I will think upon a revenge,* is the sufficient explanation,—in a great degree the sufficient justification,—(considering the then lawless state of Scotland, the complicity of the leading nobles, the hopelessness of justice)—of her later conduct whilst Queen.

The friend: In Rizzio's murder the main determinant was his efficiency in aiding Mary towards a Roman Catholic reaction, which would have deprived a large body of powerful nobles of the church lands. The death of Rizzio (Mary's most faithful friend) prevented this : the death of Darnley became necessary to secure the position gained.

A brother's hypocrite tears: Murray, in whose interest Rizzio was murdered, and whose privity to the murder (as afterwards to that of Darnley) is reasonably, though indirectly, proved, affected to shed tears on seeing his sister (10th March). Next day she learned the details of the plot, and her half-brother's share in it.

The flight: Mary then fled by a secret passage from Holyrood Palace through the Abbey Church, the royal tombs in which had been broken open by the revolutionary mob of 1559.

The Castle: Dunbar.

Man sins without shame: Read what Knox seems to have considered a defence of the murders of Beaton and Rizzio in his *History of the Reformation.*

A shame-begotten spell: So far as evidence remains, the melancholy psychological truth here noted is the true explanation of the unhappy Bothwell marriage.

SIDNEY AT ZUTPHEN

October 2 : 1586

WHERE Guelderland outspreads
Her green wide water-meads
Laced by the silver of the parted Rhine;
Where round the horizon low
The waving millsails go,
And poplar avenues stretch their pillar'd line;
That morn a clinging mist uncurl'd
Its folds o'er South-Fen town, and blotted out the world.

There, as the gray dawn broke,
Cloked by that ghost-white cloke,
The fifty knights of England sat in steel;
Each man all ear, for eye
Could not his nearest spy;
And in the mirk's dim hiding heart they feel,
—Feel more than hear,—the signal sound
Of tramp and hoof and wheel, and guns that bruise the ground.

—Sudden, the mist gathers up like a curtain, the theatre clear;
Stage of unequal conflict, and triumph purchased too dear!
Half our best treasures of gallanthood there, with axe and with glaive,
One against ten,—what of that?—We are ready for glory or grave!
There, Spain and her thousands nearing, with lightning-tongued weapons of war,
Ebro's swarthy sons, and the bands from Epirus afar;
Crescia, Gonzaga, del Vasto,—world-famous names of affright,
Veterans of iron and blood, insatiable engines of fight:—
But ours were Norris and Essex and Stanley and Willoughby grim,
And the waning Dudley star, and the star that will never be dim,
Star of Philip the peerless,—and now at height of his noon,
Astrophel!—not for thyself but for England extinguish'd too soon!

Red walls of Zutphen behind; before them, Spain in her might:—
O! 'tis not war, but a game of heroic boyish delight!

For on, like a bolt-head of steel, go the fifty, dividing
    their way,
Through the brown mail-shirts, and over,—Farnese's
    choicest array;
Over and through, and the curtel-axe flashes, the plumes
    in their pride
Sink like the larch to the hewer, a death-mown avenue
    wide:
While the foe in his stubbornness flanks them and bars
    them, with merciless aim
Shooting from musket and saker a scornful death-tongue
    of flame.
As in an autumn afar, the Six Hundred in Chersonese
    hew'd
Their road through a host, for their England and honour's
    sake wasting their blood,
Foolishness wiser than wisdom!—So these, since Azin-
    court morn,
First showing the world the calm open-eyed rashness of
    Englishmen born!

Foes ere the cloud went up, black Norris and Stanley in one
Pledge iron hands and kiss swords, each his mate's, in
    the face of the sun,
Warm with the generous heat of the battle; and Wil-
    loughby's might

To the turf bore Crescia, and lifted again,— knight
    honouring knight;
All in the hurry and turmoil :—where North, half-booted
    and rough,
Launch'd on the struggle, and Sidney struck onward, his
    cuisses thrown off,
Rash over-courage of poet and youth !—while the memo-
    ries, how
At the joust long syne She look'd on, as he triumph'd,
    were hot on his brow,
'Stella! mine own, my own star!'—and he sigh'd:—and
    towards him a flame
Shot its red signal; a shriek!—and the viewless messenger
    came;
Found the unguarded gap, the approach left bare to the
    prey,
Where through the limb to the life the death-stroke
    shatter'd a way.

    —Astrophel! England's pride!
    O stroke that, when he died,
Thrill'd through the realm,—our best, our fairest
    ta'en!
    For now the wound accurst
    Lights up death's fury-thirst;—
Yet the allaying cup, in all that pain,

Untouch'd, untasted he gives o'er
To one who lay, and watch'd with eyes that craved it
  more :—

'Take it,' he said, "'tis thine ;
'Thy need is more than mine';—
And smiled as one who looks through death to life :
—Then pass'd, true heart and brave,
Leal from birth to grave,
Beyond the precincts of earth's idle strife :—
Starbright among God's stars above ;
All mortal passion still'd in that eternal Love.

In 1585 Elizabeth, who was then aiding the United Provinces in their resistance to Spain, sent Sir Philip Sidney (born 1554) as governor of the fortress of Flushing in Zealand. The Earl of Leicester, chosen by the Queen's unhappy partiality to command the English force, named Sidney (his nephew) General of the horse. He marched thence to Zutphen in Guelderland, a town besieged by the Spaniards, in hopes of destroying a strong reinforcement which they were bringing in aid of the besiegers. The details of the rash and heroic charge which followed may be read in Motley's *History of the United Netherlands*, ch. ix.

Guelderland : in this province the Rhine divides before entering the sea : 'gliding through a vast plain.'

South-Fen : Zutphen, on the Yssel (Rhine).

The bands from Epirus : Crescia, the Epirote chief, commanded a body of Albanian cavalry.

The waning Dudley star : Leicester, who was near the end of his miserable career.

Astrophel : Sidney celebrated his love for Penelope Devereux, Lady Rich, in the series of Sonnets and Lyrics named *Astrophel and Stella:*—published after his death (1591). After, or with Shakespeare's Sonnets, this series seems to me to offer the most powerful picture of the passion of love in the whole range of our poetry.

Saker: early name for field-piece.

The Six Hundred: The Crimea in ancient days was named *Chersonesus Taurica.*

Black Norris: had been at variance with Sir W. Stanley before the engagement. Norris was one of twelve gallant brothers, whose complexion followed that of their mother, named by Elizabeth 'her ' own crow.'

North: was lying bedrid from a wound in the leg, but could not resist volunteering at Zutphen, and rode up 'with one boot on and ' one boot off.'

Cuisses:
I saw young Harry, with his beaver on,
His cuisses on his thighs : (*Henry IV,* Part I : A. iv : S. i) :— Sidney flung off his 'in a fit of chivalrous extravagance.'

At the joust: In Sonnets 41 and 53 of *Astrophel and Stella* Sidney describes how the sudden sight of Stella dazzled him as he rode in certain tournaments. In Son. 69 he cries :
I, I, O, I, may say that she is mine.

ELIZABETH AT TILBURY

September : 1588

Let them come, come never so proudly,
    O'er the green waves as giants ride;
Silver clarions menacing loudly,
    'All the Spains' on their banners wide;
High on deck of the gilded galleys
    Our light sailers they scorn below :—
We will scatter them, plague, and shatter them,
    Till their flag hauls down to their foe!
        For our oath we swear
        By the name we bear,
By England's Queen, and England free and fair,—
Her's ever and her's still, come life, come death,—
        God save Elizabeth!

Sidonía, Recalde, and Leyva
    Watch from their bulwarks in swarthy scorn,
Lords and Princes by Philip's favour ;—
    We by birthright are noble born!
Freemen born of the blood of freemen,
    Sons of Creçy and Flodden are we!

We shall sunder them, fire, and plunder them,—
    English boats on the English sea!
      And our oath we swear,
      By the name we bear,
By England's Queen, and England free and fair,—
Her's ever and her's still, come life, come death!
      God save Elizabeth!

Drake and Frobisher, Hawkins, and Howard,
    Raleigh, Cavendish, Cecil, and Brooke,
Hang like wasps by the flagships tower'd,
    Sting their way through the thrice-piled oak:—
Let them range their seven-mile crescent,
    Giant galleons, canvas wide!
Ours will harry them, board, and carry them,
    Plucking the plumes of the Spanish pride.
      For our oath we swear
      By the name we bear,
By England's Queen, and England free and fair,—
Her's ever and her's still, come life, come death!
      God save Elizabeth!

—Hath God risen in wrath and scatter'd?
    Have his tempests smote them in scorn?
Past the Orcades, dumb and tatter'd,
    'Mong sea-beasts do they drift forlorn?

We were as lions hungry for battle;
   God has made our battle his own!
God has scatter'd them, sunk, and shatter'd them:
   Give the glory to him alone!
      While our oath we swear,
      By the name we bear,
By England's Queen, and England free and fair,—
Her's ever and her's still, come life, come death!
   God save Elizabeth!

EL DORADO

1595

WHAT golden voice their golden deeds should sing
Who 'neath that flag of Hope and England sail,
The flaming zone-walls of the world to scale,
  Borne up on eagle-wing

To far horizons, 'neath translucent skies,
Beyond Atlantic, clad in fadeless green
And equatorial glory, visibly seen
  By those keen eagle eyes?

—His best,—whose song moves with that Dorian pace
Imperious, torrent fervency of words,
Words bright and brief as lightning, edged like swords,
  Yet all to perfect grace

Attuned, Aglaia's handiwork divine,
Where Freedom veils herself in Law severe,
And Beauty's lightest whisper echoes clear
  Through each consummate line.

This crown'd the conqueror's crown, when he, who now
Sups nightly with Apollo, sang the race;
Or how swift Argo cut the ocean-space
    With sharp triumphant prow;

Or how Atlantis loads the air with balm,
The purple Paradise of the purple main,
By seamen past Azorés sought in vain,
    Ring'd with eternal calm:

Lifting its pyramid of green delight
With shining summits topp'd, and snows that lie,
Nature's pure offering to the stainless sky,
    Past Himalayan height.

There, freed from our sick weight of hopes and fears,
The spirits of the just find fit abode;
Absolute peace ineffable; and the God
    Wipes from their eyes all tears.

There, friend with friend in so-long-wish'd embrace,
In rose-crown'd companies of song they move;
Star-eyed with bliss, and smiles of perfect love
    Incarnadine the face.

—Ah vision that no mortal eye may view!—
Not those whom now the Poet-Chieftain guides
By Lancerota, through the steaming tides
    From Hamoaze haven blue.

Another sight awaits them, when the mouth
Of that great Orenoque they face, who drains
Whole continents through a thousand mazy veins,
    Fed by the fertile South;

Huge serpent jaws, that endless warfare wage,
Sea-tides and inland floods well-match'd in ire;
As when of old Scamander boil'd with fire
    Breathed by Poseidon's rage:—

Or as beneath Lofoden's trembling height
The green gyrations of the tortured wave
Orbing from Islesen past Mosköe rave,
    And with main whirlpool might

Spin the frail bark that struggles in the abyss:—
Yet that indomitable heart his way
Holds, and the mariner-hearts beneath his sway
    Swell, emulous of his:—

And now the seething bar is past: The boat
Up wide Amana, islanded with palms
Twinn'd in their beauty on the mirroring calms,
  In summer peace may float;

While, right and left, a pillar'd wall of green
Screens the new world:—Such sight as glads the gaze
Of voyagers on Dart, in earlier days
  By Devon Raleigh seen,

E'en then, perchance, in memory seen afar.
—Now, sudden sunset falls; an arch of gold
In tropic fury round the west is roll'd
  For Day's retreating car,

And the sun bathes in blood, imperial gloom!
Then weaves his flashing network o'er the skies,
Making the heaven one rainbow, as he dies,
  The canopy of his tomb.

Pageant of human glory, paling soon
In truth's calm light!—as now, when, blue on blue,
The immeasurable heavens their depths renew,
  Clear'd by the sailing moon:—

And day returns :—And now the forest yields,
And Paradise is before them, (name it so),
Where far savannas stretch in golden glow
   Like England's fairest fields ;

Nor want the grace of scatter'd glades, between
Lifting green domes, or blossoming in fire ;
While living gems, on wings that cannot tire,
   With diamond flashings keen,

Emerald, and ruby, flicker o'er the flowers,
Or pass from sight in their own sunshine veil'd,
Excess of glory !—Not the Prince who sail'd
   Past the white lotos-bowers,

Hanno, from Gadés, with more hungry glance
Devour'd earth's wonders, than that roving crew,
Still pushing south through marvels ever new,
   And hearts that higher dance

With each new marvel:—Rocks, whose crest is crown'd
With forest mass'd o'er forest ; cataracts white
That from the mid-sky seem to break in might,
   Exulting as they bound

From Aromaia's breast, or the red walls
Of yet-untrod Roraima, clad in clouds
Of ceaseless steam, and silver hanging shrouds,
  Mother of myriad falls.

There, or in like asylum, unassail'd,
The Golden City, all her palace-halls
With monsters carved a-gape, huge towers and walls,
  Manóa, may lie veil'd

From Europe's curious gaze : her miles of street,
A wilderness of roof and shrine and gold,
On which the flooding fervours, as of old,
  In zenith fury beat,

Sunshine by goldshine doubled!—Vision high,
On earth unparallel'd!—Yet not to thee,
O chief for gain too eager, given to see,
  Nor any mortal eye.

Far other fate expects thee, other skies!
—O treacherous lust of gold, that steals the heart
Of heroes, counterfeiting Virtue's part,
  Fiend in an angel's guise,

Luring the adventurous breast to perilous shoals
And final shipwreck, when that golden shore
Again he touch'd, seeking the fatal ore,
  The shining bait of souls.

Ah curséd thirst! that hamper'd not alone
His fame, but dusks with a yet deeper stain
That greater other, who all Nature's reign
  From his imperial throne

Of intellectual altitude survey'd,
Interpreter of Law to all mankind,
Yet to the common light of conscience blind,
  Himself by self betray'd!

—O gifted victims, by their gifts brought low!
Consumed by their own fire!—One from his place
Of pride, law's central throne, in world-disgrace
  Thrust: piteous overthrow

Eternized by his genius!—Glory-shame
His portion for all ages!—Soul so great
Smirch'd by that meanness!—Irony of Fate
  At sport with such a fame!

—But in that fall a late revenge he found,
Raleigh, imprison'd eagle :—he who lay
By the unjust justice of that tyrannous day
        In the dark Tower-cell bound,

Our monumental Keep, each stone a page
Of England's history :—For the jealous King,
Mistrustful, chain'd his feet and clipp'd his wing,
        Whilst he, with restless rage

Beat at the bars, his poet-soul full-fill'd
With giant schemes for man afar descried ;—
A hero marr'd by piracy and pride,
        Self-blinded and self-will'd,

Till on his fate he rush'd, through lawless strife
Trapp'd in the nets of long-revengeful Spain :
And though by unjust sentence justly slain,
        Greater in death than life.

O gifted victim of a difficult age,
Train'd while the danger of the land to ruse
And greed and violence lent a vague excuse ;—
        While yet the Spanish rage,

And she, by cruel weakness to our wrong
And her's, a captive—lived,—to plague the land
With plot and peril :—While the roving band
    Of seamen sturdy-strong,

Half pirate and half patriot, might carve out
Law for themselves, 'No peace beyond the Line,'
Grenville and Drake !—But now the Orkneyan brine
    With that Castilian rout

When Ocean conquer'd the Unconquerable
Was navy-glutted, and the pride of Spain
Fell !—and lo !—Peace with all her genial train
    Returning here to dwell :

Trade that, inverting Tyrian legend, sails
Through the long mid-land lake to Sidon shore,
Or from Golconda bears a glittering store,
    Or silken-sheeny bales

From far Cambodia :—While the loom and mine
Stir with fresh life :—brown tillage scores the field
Long fallow, and new fruit the gardens yield :
    War-darken'd hearths re-shine,

And ancient Plenty smiles on all the Poor :—
Gay palace-homes, that crowd the land, their line
Of many-window'd height uplift,—the sign
      Of settled Peace secure.

And as the storm-clouds thus their threat withdraw,
To its old self the heart of England turns,
Days of Plantagenet liberty, and burns
      For Freedom and for Law :—

Free voice, free aid, free counsel :—A free throne
By freemen circled; each respecting each ;
A realm self-centred, yet with arm to reach
      Where earth's oppress'd-ones groan,

Protecting and avenging !—Peace meanwhile,
Peace East and South, to vine and olive-grove,
Or where o'er Indian seas the galliots rove,
      Once mann'd by greed and guile.

—Dream of Utopian souls !—For when the flood
Of passion by fanatic zeal is lash'd,
Creed against creed, nation 'gainst nation dash'd,
      Man's bestial thirst for blood

For blood cries out :—And lo !—from shore to shore
The fiends of war and lawlessness and hate,
And England by her sons laid desolate,
And sunset-red with gore !

Argument

St. 1-9 : Raleigh's expeditions to America in 1595 and 1617 should have been sung by Pindar, who told the voyage of Argo and described the region of the happy dead with such magnificence. St. 10-25 Raleigh's first voyage to Guiana : he ascends one branch of the Orinoco, but does not reach the supposed Golden City Manoa (26-28). St. 29-42 Raleigh's second unhappy voyage : He is paralleled with Lord Chancellor Bacon in love of wealth and in the calamities of his later life. Outline of his character. Picture of the prosperity and political development of England during the later years of Elizabeth's reign, and anticipations of the Civil War : St. 43-50.

Aglaia : one of the Graces.

Sups nightly with Apollo : The story is that at Delphi, long after the Poet's death (B.C. 442), every evening as the great Temple was closed for the night the sacristan paused and cried—*Pindar to supper with the God !*

Atlantis : A Paradise imagined by the Greeks in the Western Seas. Allusion is here made to Pindar's Second Olympian Ode and a magnificent fragment of a *Threnos*.

Hamoaze : Raleigh sailed from Plymouth on his first voyage 9th February 1595. His journal describes, rather briefly and confusedly, the tropical scenery of that branch of the Orinoco (identified by Schomburgk with the *Amana*) up which he voyaged. The Caroni, rising from the hitherto unascended red plateau of Roraima, falls

into it. The natives named Roraima 'the ever-fertile source of
' streams.' The descriptions of this region given by Humboldt
and Schomburgk have been referred to for these stanzas.

Hanno from Gadés: whence this early Phoenician explorer (cir.
470 B.C.) sailed on a coast voyage in hope to circumnavigate Africa.

A late revenge: Bacon was one of the commissioners for Raleigh's
examination when imprisoned on returning from his second voyage
to Guiana in 1617-8, and drew up the report proposing that he
should be tried again upon the alleged plot of 1603. This course,
however, was set aside in favour of executing the hitherto suspended
sentence passed on him in that year at Winchester. The details
of the case will be found ably and fully set forth in Mr. R. Gardiner's
' Prince Charles and the Spanish Marriage,' vol. i : ch. ii. There
is, of course, not a little to admire and much to pity in Raleigh's
career ; on the latter part of which the truest criticism might be,
that he could not, or would not, perceive the wholly changed position of England after the ruin of the prepotent influence of Spain.
Yet if we put aside the natural but judgment-perverting prepossession in favour of genius, the evidence proves, fully and convincingly,
that the sentence of death passed (although Raleigh's conduct
cannot be wholly cleared) in 1603, was as undeserved as that of
death for his management of the expedition in 1617 would have
been merited. Hence the phrase used, 'by unjust sentence justly
slain.'

She . . . a captive: Mary of Scotland.

Tyrian legend: Of voyages beyond the Mediterranean westward.

Palace-homes: The entire disappearance of the castellar element
from our country-houses is hardly seen before the last quarter of the
sixteenth century.

PRINCE CHARLES AT THE LOUVRE

February: 1623

From gay Montreuil in the dawning
Gaily they ride on their way,
And the spirit of youth around them
Is fresh with the freshness of day.

Over wide brown heaving billows
Of cornland and gorseland they go,
Where Spring in the bud is sleeping,
And life in the roots below.

Each waits its own season, springtide,
And life, and love, to break out :—
The heart of the Prince stirs vaguely
Poised 'tween desire and doubt.

For she who awaits his wooing
In Aranjuez gardens green
Is but as a vision of dreamland,
A saint in her heaven unseen.

Now, as one who seeks high Monserrat
He rides to her shrine through France:
And turns him aside to Paris,
For the Queen is holding a dance;

And his eyes would feast on the splendour
Of the royal cousins fair;
Disguised as a pilgrim errant
Who sees what he may not share.

—O spring-tide of life! In the bosom
The buds of first-love lie:
But the sunbeam they wait, or the shower,
To go forth with joy to the sky:—

And we see the fairest of fair ones,
The heart's own ownest-to-be,—
A child in her maiden beauty,
—And know not that this is she!

For the great Magician, he glories
To lead us in paths unknown,
That all may confess him sovereign,
And bow to King Love alone.

—Nineteen fair ones he look'd on
In the measured masque as they trod
But his eyes were seal'd and dazzled
By the blinding blindfold God.

He look'd and pass'd on his voyage
To the shrine of Castilian pride:
Nor knew he what quick young glances
That island stranger had spied:—

Nor who in his rosy raiment
And rose-flame breath was there,
Watching his victim-children
Play out their play unaware:—

Nor how with a darker crimson
The sky was gathering afar:
The blue steel-gleam of the lightning,—
The red fall of a royal star!

From gay Montreuil: See Appendix.
Aranjuez: A favourite palace of Spanish royalty on the Tagus, south of Madrid.
Monserrat: A celebrated place of pilgrimage in north-eastern Spain.

AT BEMERTON

1630-1633

Sick with the strife of tongues, the blustering hate
Of frantic Party raving o'er the realm,
Sonorous insincerities of debate,
And jealous factions snatching at the helm,
And Out o'er-bidding In with graceless strife,
Selling the State for votes :—O happy fields,
I cried, where Herbert, by the world misprized,
      Found in his day the life
That no unrest or disappointment yields,
Vergilian vision here best realized!

His memory is Peace: and peace is here ;—
The eternal lullaby of the level brook,
With bird-like chirpings mingled, glassy-clear ;
The narrow pathway to the yew-clipp'd nook ;
Trim lawn, familiar to the pensive feet ;
The long gray walls he raised :—A household nest
Where Hope and firm-eyed Faith and heavenly Love
      Made human love more sweet ;
While,—earth's rare visitant from the choirs above,—
Urania's holy steps the cottage blest.

Peace there:—and peace upon the house of God,
The little road-side church that room-like stands
Crouching entrench'd in slopes of daisy sod,
And duly deck'd by Herbert-honouring hands:—
Cell of detachment! Shrine to which the heart
Withdraws, and all the roar of life is still;
Then sinks into herself, and finds a shrine
    Within the shrine apart;
Alone with God, as on the Arabian hill
Man knelt in vision to the All-divine!

—Thrice happy they,—and know their happiness,—
Who read the soul's star-orbit Heaven-ward clear;
Not roving comet-like through doubt and guess,
But 'neath their feet tread nescient pride and fear;
Scan the unseen with sober certainty,
God's hill above Himalah;—Love green earth
With deeper, truer love, because the blue
    Of Heaven around they see;—
Who in the death-gasp hail man's second birth,
And yield their loved ones with a brief adieu!

—Thee, too, esteem I happy in thy death,
Poet! while yet peace was, and thou might'st live
Unvex'd in thy sweet reasonable faith,
The gracious creed that knows how to forgive:—

Not narrowing God to self,—the common bane
Of sects, each man his own small oracle ;
Not losing innerness in external rite ;
  A worship pure and plain,
Yet liberal to man's heaven-imbreathed delight
In all that sound can hint, or beauty tell.

A golden moderation !—which the wise
Then highest rate, when fury-factions roar,
And folly's choicest fools the most despise :—
—O happy Poet ! laid in peace before
Rival intolerants each 'gainst other flamed,
And flames were slaked in blood, and all the grace
Of life before that sad illiterate gloom
  Puritan, fled ashamed :
While, as the red moon lifts her turbid face,
Titanic features on the horizon loom !

 George Herbert's brief career as a parish priest was passed at Bemerton, a pretty village near Salisbury in the vale of the Avon. His parsonage, with its garden running down to the stream, and the little church across the road in which he lies buried, remain comparatively unchanged since he lived and mused and wrote his Poems within these precincts. The justly-famous *Temple* was published shortly after his death by his friend Nicholas Ferrar.
 Arabian hill : Mount Sinai.
 Titanic features : See *A Churchyard in Oxfordshire*, st. iii.

PRINCESS ANNE

November 5 : 1640

Harsh words have been utter'd and written on her, Henrietta the Queen :
She was young in a difficult part, on a cruel and difficult scene :—
Was it strange she should fail? that the King overmuch should bow down to her will?
—So of old with the women, God bless them !—it was, so will ever be still !
Rash in counsel and rash in courage, she aided and marr'd
The shifting tides of the fight, the star of the Stuarts ill-starr'd.
In her the false Florentine blood,—in him the bad strain of the Guise ;
Hypocritic ambition against them, and crazy fanatic lies :—
As a bird by the fowlers o'ernetted, she shuffles and changes her ground ;
All wiles lawful in war, and the foe unscrupulous round !

Woman-like overbelieving Herself and the Cause and the Man,
Fights with two-edged intrigue, suicidal, plan upon plan;
Till the law of this world had its way, and she fled,—like a frigate unsail'd,
Unmasted, unflagg'd,—to her land: and the greater power prevail'd.

But it was not thus, not thus, in the years of thy spring-tide, O Queen,
When thy children came in their beauty, and all their future unseen:
When the kingdom had wealth and peace, one smile o'er the face of the land:
England, too happy, if thou could'st thy happiness understand!
As those over Etna who slumber, and under them rankles the fire,
At her side was the gallant King, her first-love, her girlhood's desire,
And around her, best jewels and brightest to deck the steps of the throne,
Three golden heads, three fair little maids, in their nursery shone.

'As the mother, so be the daughters,' they say:—nor
    could mother wish more
For her own, than men saw in the Queen's, ere the
    rosebud-dawning was o'er,
Heart-wise and head-wise, a joy to behold, as they
    knelt for her kiss,—
Best crown of a woman's life, her true vocation and
    bliss!—
But the flowers were pale and frail, and the mother watch'd
    them with dread,
As the sunbeams play'd round the room on each gay,
    glistening head.

Anne in that garden of childhood grew nearest Elizabeth:
    she
Tenderly tended and loved her, a babe with a babe on
    her knee:
Slight and white from the cradle was Anne; a floweret
    born
Rathe, out of season, a rose that peep'd out when the
    hedge was in thorn.
'Why should it be so with us?' thought Elizabeth oft;
    for in her
The soul 'gainst the body protesting, was but more keenly
    astir:

'As saplings stunted by forest around o'ershading, we two:
'What work for our life, my mother,' she said, 'is left us to do?
'Or is't from the evil to come, the days without pleasure, that God
'Is wishing to spare us, over our childhood outstretching the rod?'
—So she, from her innocent heart; in all things seeing the best
With the wholesome spirit of childhood; to God submitting the rest:
Not seeing the desolate years, the dungeon of Carisbrook drear;
Eyes dry-glazed with fever, and none to lend even a tear!
Now, all her heart to the little one goes; for, day upon day,
As a rosebud in canker, she shrinks and pales, and the cough has its way.
And the gardens of Richmond on Thames, the fine blythe air of the vale
Stay not the waning pulse, and the masters of science fail.
Then the little footsteps are faint, and a child may take her with ease;
As the flowers a babe flings down she is spread on Elizabeth's knees,

Slipping back to the cradle-life, in her wasting weakness and pain:
And the sister prays and smiles and watches the sister in vain.

So she watch'd by the bed all night, and the lights were yellow and low,
And a cold blue blink came in from the park that was sheeted in snow:
And the frost of the passing hour, when souls from the body divide,
The Sarsar-wind of the dawn, crept into the palace, and sigh'd.
And the child just turn'd her head towards Elizabeth there as she lay,
And her little hands came together in haste, as though she would pray:
And Elizabeth call'd 'O Father, why does she look at me so?
'Will it soon be better for Anne? her face is all in a glow':—
But the mother propp'd up the downward head, and whisper'd to pray
To the Father in heaven, 'the one she likes best, my baby, to say':

And the soul hover'd yet o'er the lips, as a dove when her pinions are spread,
And the light of the after-life came again in her eyes, and she said;
'For my long prayer it is not time; for my short one I think I have breath;
'*Lighten mine eyes, O Lord, that I sleep not the sleep of death.*'
—O! into life, fair child, as she pray'd, her innocence slept!
'It *is* better for her,' they said:—and knelt, and kiss'd her, and wept.

In her: Henrietta's mother was by birth Mary de' Medici; the great-grandmother of Charles was Mary of Guise.

'With Charles I,' says Ranke, 'nothing was more seductive 'than secrecy. The contradictions in his conduct entangled him 'in embarrassments, in which his declarations, if always true in the 'sense he privately gave them, were only a hair's-breadth removed 'from actual, and even from intentional, untruth.'—Whether traceable to descent, or to the evil influence of Buckingham and the intriguing atmosphere of the Spanish marriage-negotiations, this, (though his antagonists' conduct disentitles them from pleading it against him), is, unquestionably, the one great blot on the character of Charles I.

Crazy lies: It will be enough to quote one. In the solemn declaration of the Commons (1648) against further treating with Charles, 'they more than insinuate his participation in the murder 'of his father by Buckingham:' (Hallam: *Const. Hist.* ch. x).

When the kingdom : See Clarendon's description of England during this period, 'enjoying the greatest calm and the fullest 'measure of felicity that any people in any age for so long time 'together have been blessed with.'—'We may acknowledge without 'hesitation,' says Hallam, commenting on this passage, 'that the 'kingdom had grown during this period into remarkable prosperity 'and affluence': (*Const. Hist.* ch. viii).

Three golden heads : Mary, the second child of Charles and Henrietta, was born Nov. 4, 1631 : Elizabeth, Dec. 28, 1635 : Anne, Mar. 17, 1637. The last two were feeble from infancy. Consumption soon showed itself in Anne, and her short life, passed at Richmond, closed in November, 1640. For her last words, we are indebted to Fuller, who adds : 'This done, the little lamb gave 'up the ghost.'

The affection and care of the royal parents is well attested. 'Their arrival,' when visiting the nursery, 'was the signal of a 'general rejoicing.'

In the latter portion of this piece I have ventured, it will be seen, on an ideal treatment. The main facts, and the words of the dear child, are historical :—for the details I appeal to any mother who has suffered similar loss whether they could have been much otherwise.

Not seeing : See the *Captive Child.*

The frost : It is noticed that death often occurs at the turn between night and day, when the atmosphere is wont to be at the coldest.

AFTER CHALGROVE FIGHT

June: 1643

FLAGS crape-smother'd and arms reversed,
With one sad volley lay him to rest:
Lay him to rest where he may not see
This England he loved like a lover accursed
By lawlessness masking as liberty,
By the despot in Freedom's panoply drest:—
Bury him, ere he be made duplicity's tool and slave,
Where he cannot see the land that he could not save!
    Bury him, bury him, bury him
       With his face downward!

    Chalgrove! Name of patriot pain!
    O'er thy fresh fields that summer pass'd
    The brand of war's red furnace blast,
Till heaven's soft tears wash'd out the blackening
       stain;—
Wash'd out and wept;—But could not so restore
       England's gallant son:
       Ere the fray was done
The stately head bow'd down; shatter'd; his warfare o'er.

Bending to the saddle-bow
With leaden arm that idle hangs,
Faint with the lancing torture-pangs,
He drops the rein; he lets the battle go :—
There, where the wife of his first love he woo'd
Moving for retreat ;—
Memories bitter-sweet
Through death's fast-rising mist in beauty now renew'd.

Then, as those who drown, perchance,
And see their years in sudden gleam
Flash by, a morning moment's dream,
Life's spring-sweet hours before him go and glance;
The hearth-side smile; the fragrance of the fields:
—Now, war's iron knell
Clanging heaven to hell,
Whilst o'er the realm her scourge the vengeful Fury wields!

Doth he now the day lament
When those who stemm'd despotic might
O'erstrode the bounds of law and right,
And through the land the torch of ruin sent?
Or that great rival statesman as he stood
Lion-faced and grim,
Hath he sight of him,
Strafford—the meteor-axe—the fateful Hill of Blood?

—Heroes both! by passion led,
 In days perplex'd 'tween new and old,
 Each at his will the realm to mould;
This, basing sovereignty on the single head,
This, on the many voices of the Hall:—
  Each for his own creed
  Prompt to die at need:
His side of England's shield each saw, and took for all.

  Heroes both! For Order one
  And one for Freedom dying!—We
  May judge more justly both, than ye
Could, each, his brother, ere the strife was done!
—O Goddess of that even scale and weight,
  In whose heart alone
  Mercy sets her throne,
This hero-dirge to thee I vow and dedicate!

  —Turning now,—the foe is by,—
  Through Hazeley mead the warrior goes,
  And hardly fords the brook that flows
Bearing to Thame its cool, sweet, summer-cry.
Here take thy final rest, thy long release!
  By death's mercy-doom
  Hid from ills to come,
Great soul, and greatly vex'd, Hampden!—depart in peace!

In the heart of the fields he loved and the hills,
Look your last, and lay him to rest,
With the faded flower, the wither'd grass;
Where the blood-face of war and the myriad ills
Of England dear like phantoms pass
And touch not the soul that is with the Blest.
Bury him in the night and peace of the holy grave,
Where he cannot see the land that he could not save!
Bury him, bury him, bury him
With his face downward!

John Hampden met his death at Chalgrove in an attempt to check the raids which Prince Rupert was making from Oxford. Struck at onset in the shoulder by two carabine balls, he rode off before the action was ended by Hazeley towards Thame, finding it impossible to reach Pyrton, the home of his father-in-law. The body was carried to his own house amid the woods and hills of the Chiltern country, and buried in the church close by.

With his face downward: This was the dying request of some high-minded Spaniard of old, unwilling, even in the grave, as it were, to look on the misfortunes of his country.

Doth he now: See Appendix.

O'erstrode the bounds: 'After every allowance has been made,' says Hallam, speaking of the Long Parliament from a date so early as August, 1641, 'he must bring very heated passions to the records ' of those times, who does not perceive in the conduct of that body ' a series of glaring violations, not only of positive and constitu- ' tional, but of those higher principles which are paramount to all ' immediate policy': (*Const. Hist.* ch. ix).

The axe: For a full and impartial history of Strafford's trial we must wait till Mr. R. Gardiner's book reaches that period. A brief and clear account, meanwhile, will be found in Ranke (B. viii): who deals dispassionately and historically with an event much obscured by declamation in popular narratives. Even in Hallam's hand the balance seems here to waver a little.

Heroes both: See Appendix.   *Each his side:* See Appendix.

A CHURCHYARD IN OXFORDSHIRE

September : 1643

SWEET air and fresh; glades yet unsear'd by hand
Of Midas-finger'd Autumn, massy-green;
Bird-haunted nooks between,
Where feathery ferns, a fairy palmgrove, stand,
Our English-Eastern band :—
While e'en the stealthy squirrel o'er the grass
Beside me to the beech-clump dares to pass :—
In this still precinct of the happy dead,
The sanctuary of silence,—Blessed they!
I cried, who 'neath the gray
Peace of God's house, each in his mounded bed
Sleep safe, nor reck how the great world runs on;
Peasant with noble here alike unknown.

Unknown, unnamed beneath one turf they sleep,
Beneath one sky, one heaven-uplifted sign
Of love assured, divine :
While o'er each mound the quiet mosses creep,
The silent dew-pearls weep :

—Fit haven-home for thee, O gentle heart
Of Falkland! all unmeet to find thy part
In those tempestuous times of canker'd hate
When Wisdom's finest touch, and, by her side,
Forbearance generous-eyed
To fix the delicate balance of the State
Were needed;—King or Nation, which should hold
Supreme supremacy o'er the kingdoms old.

—God's heroes, who? . . . Not most, or likeliest, he
Whom iron will cramps to one narrow road,
Driving him like a goad,
Till all his heart decrees seems God's decree;
That worst hypocrisy
When self cheats self, and conscience at the wheel
Herself is steer'd by passion's blindfold zeal;
A nether-world archangel! Through whose eyes
Flame the red mandates of remorseless might;
A gloom of lurid light
That holds no commerce with the crystal skies;
Like those rank fires that o'er the fen-land flee,
Or on the mast-head sign the wrath to be.

As o'er that ancient weird Arlesian plain
Where Zeus hail'd boulder-stones on the giant crew,

And changed to stone, or slew,
No bud may burgeon in Spring's gracious rain,
No blade of grass or grain:
—So bare, so scourged, a prey to chaos cast
The wisest despot leaves his realm at last!
Though for the land he toil'd with iron will,
Earnest to reach persuasion's goal through power,
The fruit without the flower!
And pray'd and wrestled to charm good from ill;
Waking perchance, or not, in death,—to find
Man fights a losing fight who fights mankind!

And as who in that Theban avenue,
Sphinx ranged by Sphinx, goes awestruck, nor may find
His entrance to the mind
Set in their granite calm:—so we no clue
Can trace, to lead us through
That labyrinthine soul which, day by day
Changing, yet kept one long imperious way:
Strong in his weakness; confident, yet forlorn;
Waning and waxing; diamond-keen, or dull,
As that star Wonderful,
Mira, in Cetus, dying and reborn:—
Blissful or baleful, yet a Power throughout,
Throned in dim altitude o'er the common rout.

Alas, great chief! The pity of it!—For he
Lay on his unlamented bier; his life
Wreck'd on that futile strife
To wed things alien by heaven's decree,
Sword-sway with liberty:—
Coercing, not protecting;—for the Cause
Smiting with iron heel on England's laws
Intolerant tolerance! Soul that could not trust
Its finer instincts; self-compell'd to run
The blood-path once begun,
And murder mercy with a sad 'I must!'
Great lion-heart by guile and coarseness marr'd;
By his own heat a hero warp'd and scarr'd.

Despot despite himself!—And when the cry
Moan'd up from England, dungeon'd in that drear
Sectarian atmosphere,
With glory he gilt her chains; in Spanish sky
Flaunting the Red Cross high;—
Wars, just or unjust, ill or well design'd,
Urged with the will that masters weak mankind.
—God's hammer this, not hero!—Forged to break
The land, not minister healing and relief;
Philistia's child and chief:—
To all who worship power for power's own sake,

Strength for itself, Success, the vulgar test,
Fit idol of bent knee, and servile breast!

—O in the party plaudits of the crowd
Glorious, if this be glory!—o'er that shout
A small still voice breathes out
With subtle sweetness silencing the loud
Hoarse vaunting of the proud,—
A song of exaltation for the vale,
And how the mountain from his height shall fail!
How God's true heroes, since this earth began,
Go sackcloth-clad through scourge and sword and scorn,
Crown'd with the bitter thorn,
Down-trampled by man's heel as foes to man,
And whispering *Eli, Eli!* as they die,—
Martyrs of truth and Saint Humility.

These conquer in their fall: Persuasion flies
Wing'd, from their grave: The hearts of men are turn'd
To worship what they burn'd:
Owning the sway of Love's long-suffering eyes,
Love's sweet self-sacrifice;
The might of gentleness; the subduing force
Of wisdom on her mid-way measured course
Gliding;—not torrent-like with fury spilt,

Impetuous, o'er Himalah's rifted side,
To ravage blind and wide,
And leave a lifeless wreck of parching silt;—
Gliding by tower and thorpe and grange and lea
In tranquil transit to the eternal sea.

—Children of Light!—If, in the slow-paced course
Of vital change, your work seem incomplete,
Your conquest-hour defeat,
Won by mild compromise, by the invisible force
That owns no earthly source;
Yet to all time your gifts to man endure,
God being with you, and the victory sure!
For though with Gods the Giants in the fight
May wrestle, Strength 'gainst Beauty; yet the Soul
Darts on and clasps the goal,
And Wisdom triumphs by her proper might:
—Thus far on earth! . . . But, ah!—from these dim eyes
Aloof, above, the crowning moment lies!

Envoy

—Seal'd of that holy band,
Rest here, beneath the foot-fall hushing sod,
Wrapt in the peace of God,
While summer burns above thee; while the land

Disrobes; till pitying snow
Covers her bareness; till fresh Spring-winds blow,
And the sun-circle rounds itself again :—
Whilst England cries in vain
For thy wise temperance, Lucius !—But thine ear
Our violent-impotent fever-restless cry,
The faction-yells of triumph, will not hear :
—Only the thrush on high
And wood-dove's moaning sweetness make reply.

Lucius Cary, second Viscount Falkland, may perhaps be defined as at once the most poetically chivalrous and the most philosophically moderate amongst all who took part in the pre-restoration struggles. He was killed in the royal army at the first battle of Newbury, Sep. 20, 1643, aged but 33 years, and buried, without mark or memorial, in the church of Great Tew (North Oxfordshire), the manor of which he owned.

English Eastern: The common brake-fern and its allies seem to betray tropical sympathies by their late appearance and sensitiveness to autumnal frost.

King or nation: See Appendix.

A nether-world archangel: This phrase was suggested in part by the beautiful miniature-portrait of Cromwell prefixed to Mr. Carlyle's original edition of his *Life and Letters;* a book to which I am also indebted for a large portion of the materials whence the picture here, and in *The Return of Law,* drawn of the Protector has been framed. This picture, and that of Lord Bacon in *El Dorado,* differ widely from those presented respectively by Messrs. Spedding and Carlyle. But it is the peculiar value of such elaborate and carefully prepared repertories as we owe to these editors that, if their own notes and elucidations do not convince an unprejudiced reader, (indeed, often assist him materially towards a contrary conclusion), the actual words and writings of the great men in question are set forth so fully and so clearly that a real and independent judgment upon them is rendered possible :—a result of which the essay-written style of history does not admit.

That Arlesian plain: The *Crau*, lying between Arles and the sea, is a bare and malarious tract of great size covered with shingle and boulders. Aeschylus describes it as a 'snow-shower of round 'stones,' which Zeus rained down in aid of Heracles, who was contending with the Ligurians. This legend connects itself with his return from the expedition against Geryon at Mount Abas.

Mira: A star in the *Whale*, conspicuous for its singular and rapid changes of apparent size.

The Cause: After passing through several phases this word, in Cromwell's mouth, with the common logic of tyranny, became simply a synonym for personal rule.

Smiting with iron heel: The terrorism of Cromwell's government, and the almost universal hatred which it inspired, are described with his usual force and fairness by Hallam. 'To govern 'according to law may sometimes be an usurper's wish, but can 'seldom be in his power. The protector abandoned all thought of 'it. . . . All illusion was now (1655) gone, as to the pretended 'benefits of the civil war. It had ended in a despotism, compared 'to which all the illegal practices of former kings, all that had cost 'Charles his life and crown, appeared as dust in the balance.'

The blood-path: The trials under which Gerard and Vowel were executed in 1654, Slingsby and Hewit in 1658, are the most flagrant instances of Cromwell's perversion of justice, and contempt for the old liberties of England. But they do not stand alone. Lord Capel, as Ranke points out, was executed in 1649, although he had surrendered conditionally, and, as he believed, as a prisoner of war with security for life. But his moral worth and weight in the country having compelled Cromwell to declare that he 'would 'always be a thorn in the side of Parliament,' it was politic to destroy him: 'those in power,' adds Ranke (xi: 1), 'appearing to 'have formed the resolution to rid themselves of all men of mark 'who might ever be capable of resisting them.'

Guile and coarseness: 'A certain coarse good nature and affabi-'lity that covered the want of conscience, honour, and humanity: 'quick in passion, but not vindictive, and averse to unnecessary 'crimes,' is the deliberate summing-up of the most judicially gifted writer, and he also, inferior to none in the love of liberty, who has hitherto honoured the long roll of our historians (Hallam, *Const. Hist.* ch. x).

With glory he gilt: See Appendix.

Philistia's child: See Mr. M. Arnold's finely discriminative Essay on Falkland.

MARSTON MOOR

July 2 : 1644

O, SUMMER-HIGH that day the sun
His chariot drove o'er Marston wold:
A rippling sea of amber wheat
That floods the moorland vale with gold.

With harvest light the valley laughs,
The sheaves of hope in sunshine sleep;—
But full the crop and red the swathes
Ere night the scythes of Death shall reap!

Then thick and fast o'er all the moor
The redden'd sabre-lightnings fly;
And thick and fast the death-bolts dash,
And thunder-peals to peals reply.

Beneath the crimson-arching dome
Went up the roar of mortal foes:—
But o'er a deathly peace the moon
In silver silence sailing rose.

Sweet hour, when heaven is nearest home,
And children's kisses close the day!
O disaccord with nature's calm,
Unholy requiem of the fray!

White maiden Queen that sail'st above,
Thy dew-tears on the fallen fling,—
The blighted wreaths of civil strife,
The war that can no triumph bring!

—O pale with that deep pain of those
Who cannot save, yet must foresee,—
Surveying all the ills to flow
From that too-victor victory;

When 'gainst the unwisely guided King
The too-imperious leader stood,
And law and right and peace went down
In that red sea of brothers' blood;—

O long, long, long the years, fair Maid,
Before thy patient eye shall view
The shrine of England's law restored,
Her homes their ancient peace renew!

The day: The actual fight lay between 7 and 9 p.m.

Too-victor victory: At Naseby, says Hallam,—and the remark, (though Charles was not personally present), is equally true of Marston Moor,—' Fairfax and Cromwell triumphed, not only over ' the king and the monarchy, but over the parliament and the ' nation.'

Unwisely guided: ' Never would it have been wiser, in Rupert,' remarks Ranke, ' to avoid a decisive battle than at that moment. ' But he held that the king's letter not only empowered, but in- structed him to fight.'

Red sea: ' The slaughter was deadly, for Cromwell had for- ' bidden quarter being given': (*Ranke,* ix : 3).

THE FUGITIVE KING

August 7 : 1645

Cold gray cloud on the hill-tops,
Cold buffets of hill-side rain :—
As a bird that they hunt on the mountains,
The king, he turns from Rhôs lane :
A writing of doom on his forehead,
His eyes wan-wistful and dim ;
For his comrades seeking a shelter :
But earth has no shelter for him !

Gray silvery gleam of armour,
White ghost of a wandering king !
No sound but the iron-shod footfall
And the bridle-chains as they ring :
Save where the tears of heaven,
Shed thick o'er the loyal hills,
Rush down in a hoarse-tongued torrent
A roar of approaching ills.

But now with a sweeping curtain,
In a solid wall comes the rain,
And the troop draw bridle and hide them
In the Bush by the stream-side plain.
King Charles smiled sadly and gently;
''Tis the Beggar's Bush,' said he;
'For I of England am beggar'd,
'And her beggars may pity me.'

—O safe in the fadeless fir-tree
The squirrel may nestle and hide;
And in God's own dwelling the sparrow
Safe with her nestlings abide:—
But he goes homeless and friendless,
And manlike abides his doom;
For he knows a king has no refuge
Betwixt the throne and the tomb.

And the purple-robed braes of Alban,
The glory of stream and of plain,
The Holyrood halls of his birthright
Charles ne'er will look on again:—
And the land he loved well, not wisely,
Will almost grudge him a grave:
Then weep, too late, in her folly,
The dark Dictator's slave!

This incident occurred during the attempt made by Charles, in the dark final days of his struggle, to march from South Wales with the hope of joining Montrose in Scotland. He appears to have halted for the night of Aug. 6, 1645, at Old Radnor: and 'the ' name of *Rails Yat* (Royal gate) still points out the spot where, on ' the following morning, he left the Rhôs Lane for the road which ' brought him to shelter at Beggar's Bush': a name which is reported to be still preserved. See the *Memorials of the Civil War in Herefordshire* by the Mess. Webb (1879):—a singularly interesting and valuable contribution to the detailed knowledge of that period. And it is in such detailed statements, not in the eloquent rhetoric of party declamation, that a true picture of the great civil war and its miseries must be looked for.

THE CAPTIVE CHILD

September 8 : 1650

CHILD in girlhood's early grace,
Pale white rose of royal race,
Flower of France, and England's flower,
What dost here at twilight hour
Captive bird in castle-hold,
Picture-fair and calm and cold,
Cold and still as marble stone
In gray Carisbrook alone?
—Fold thy limbs and take thy rest,
Nestling of the silent nest!

Ah fair girl! So still and meek,
One wan hand beneath her cheek,
One on the holy texts that tell
Of God's love ineffable;—
Last dear gift her father gave
When, before to-morrow's grave,

THE VISIONS OF ENGLAND

By no unmanly grief unmann'd,
To his little orphan band
In that stress of anguish sore
He bade farewell evermore.

Doom'd, unhappy King! Had he
Known the pangs in store for thee,
Known the coarse fanatic rage
That,—despite her flower-soft age,
Maidenhood's first blooming fair,—
Fever-struck in the imprison'd air
As rosebud on the dust-hill thrown
Cast a child to die alone,—
He had shed, with his last breath,
Bitterer tears than tears of death!

As in her infant hour she took
In her hand the pictured book
Where Christ beneath the scourger bow'd,
Crying 'O poor man!' aloud,
And in baby tender pain
Kiss'd the page, and kiss'd again,
While the happy father smiled
On his sweet warm-hearted child;
—So now to him, in Carisbrook lone,
All her tenderness has flown.

Oft with a child's faithful heart
She has seen him act his part;
Nothing in his life so well
Gracing him as when he fell;
Seen him greet his bitter doom
As the mercy-message Home;
Seen the scaffold and the shame,
The red shower that fell like flame;
Till the whole heart within her died,
Dying in fancy by his side.

—Statue-still and statue-fair
Now the low wind may lift her hair,
Motionless in lip and limb;
E'en the fearful mouse may skim
O'er the window-sill, nor stir
From the crumb at sight of her;
Through the lattice unheard float
Summer blackbird's evening note;—
E'en the sullen foe would bless
That pale utter gentleness.

—Eyes of heaven, that pass and peep,
Do not question if she sleep!
She has no abiding here,
She is past the starry sphere;

Kneeling with the children sweet
At the palm-wreathed altar's feet;
—Innocents who died like thee,
Heaven-ward through man's cruelty,
To the love-smiles of their Lord
Borne through pain and fire and sword.

Elizabeth, second daughter of Charles I and Henrietta Maria, was born on Innocents' Day, 1635. The incident recounted in Stanza iv occurred in 1637. She had been taken on a visit to Hampton Court to her mother, who wished her to be present at her vesper-service, 'when Elizabeth, not yet two years old, became 'very restless. To quiet her a book of devotion was shown to 'her.' The King, when the Queen drew his attention, said, 'She 'begins young!'

This tale is told by Mrs. Green, in her excellent *Princesses of England*, (London, 1855),—a book deserving to be better known, —on the authority of the Envoy, Con.

The first grief of a very happy and promising childhood may have been the loss of her sister Anne in 1640. But by 1642, the evils of the time began to press upon Princess Elizabeth: her mother's departure from England was followed by her own capture by order of the Parliament; her confinement under conditions of varying severity; and the final farewell to her father, Jan. 29, 1649.

From that time her life was overshadowed by the sadness of her father's death, her own isolation, and her increasing feebleness of health. She seems to have been a singularly winning and intelligent girl, and she hence found or inspired affection in several of the guardians successively appointed to take charge of her. But if she had not been thus marked by beauty of nature, our indignant disgust would hardly be less at the brutal treatment inflicted by the Puritan-Independent authorities upon this child:—at the refusal of her prayer to be sent to her elder sister Mary, in Holland; at the careless removal to Carisbrook in 1650; at the solitude in which she was left to die.—Yet it is not she who most merits pity.

THE MOURNING MUSES

1650-1660

A RAGGED-raimented girl in vision I saw,—
Where the waters of Thames in silvery smoothness roll,
And the walls that of yore were the homes of laughter and awe
Raised and quell'd at the will of the lords of the soul
Marlowe and Shakespeare and Fletcher, are silent and bare,—
Wander, with inward gaze beholding the summers that were.

With a tangle of pale-gold hair o'er a forehead white,
And a pale-green bay-crown that slips its leaves on the way,
And eyes that with sudden tears of childhood are light,
And hands amid broken harp-strings that linger and play,
She goes by bank-side, the maid, and murmurs—How long
How long shall this tyranny be, O my children, this silence of song?

From the sunny south Acropolis slope and the stage
Where the sightless king at Colonus sate in his pain,
When ye fled, O my children! the night of a barbarous age,
'Neath a colder a bolder heaven renewing your reign,
Changing Ilissus for Avon, your glory broke forth
As the Palm-Bird renascent from incense and flame, and blazed out o'er the North.

Then the world in its height and might, its joyance and tears,
By the poet's mirror was vision'd, a living array
Many-hued; and mankind saw their by-past opulent years
By a magic truer than truth come forth to the day,
And beheld their own life in that pageant of life go by,
In the golden Elizabeth days, when the heart of England was high.

Then the giant Athenian Three beckon'd-in by their side
And crown'd with their ivy a Fourth, their co-equal afar;
And the lyre of another was sounding his lyrics in pride,
A Comus-music, a song of the morning-star :—

When the fog fanatic came down, and beauty was
    blurr'd;
The sapphire dull'd from the sky; the Muses' music
    unheard.

And as Flora her smile withdraws, when a cloud o'er
    the sun
  Lengthens its veil, and the blossom-chalices close,
  So the Muses, the light-wing'd, the smiling, from England are gone,
  Or hide lithe limbs in some dell,—reluctant repose:—
  Till the death-fume of tyranny lifts, and the heavens
    are blue,
And the music of life streams down and the smiles of
    Phoebus anew.

  But I Mnemosyné wander, and still as I go
  The departed treasures I see, the love-feasts of the eye;
  The *Pearl* and the *Peace;* Titianic glory and glow;
  The tints that burn, the beauty that never can die;—
  Beauty of tower'd height and cloister and spire, ·
Now roofless and bare to the moon, or hot with barbarian
    fire.

  A cry of Freedom I hear,—not freedom for Light,
  For the sullen saints over merry England to lour;

Reaction duty-disguised, a step backward to night,
A realm of the sword, millennium of ignorant power!
And I sigh for the day-star of Peace, the joy-freedom! How long
Shall this darkness of Egypt endure, O my children! this silence of song?

Bankside: Of the Thames by Southwark. Here the great theatres of the great age of our drama, from Marlowe to Fletcher, stood. All theatrical diversions were proscribed by the Puritan party in the Long Parliament; 'the playhouses were to be dis-'mantled, the spectators fined, the actors whipped at the cart's 'tail': (*Macaulay*, Ch. ii). This suppression was re-enforced by Cromwell in 1655.

South Acropolis slope: on which stood the great Theatre of Dionysos. The play alluded to is the *Oedipus Colonaeus* of Sophocles.

Comus-music: Properly, the music of a rejoicing dance and revel. —Milton's *Comus*, with his lyrical poems, was published in 1646.

The Muses . . . are gone: There is an almost entire dearth in the publication of poetry (as distinct from the re-publication) during the time of the Commonwealth. H. Vaughan's *Olor* and *Silex* (1651 and 1650-5), Bishop King's poems (anonymously), 1657, Chamberlayne's *Pharonnida* (1659), are the most noteworthy exceptions.

The departed treasures: See Appendix.

The Pearl *and the* Peace: Famous pictures by Raphael and Rubens, sold in the King's collection by order of Parliament in 1653.

Titian's *Entombment* and *Emmaus*, now among the glories of the Louvre, were lost to us at the same time.

THE WRECK OF THE ADMIRAL

A Tale of Prince Rupert

September 30 : 1651

SEVENTY league from Terceira they lay
  In the mid Atlantic straining;
And inch upon inch as she settles they know
  The leak on the Admiral gaining.

O gap that greedily sucks-in death!
  O signal-waft idly waving!
O shouts by their billow-rock'd consort unheard,
  Overnoised in the tempest's raving!

And unheard the farewells that are flung on the gale,
  And brother is parted from brother,
For the gallant chief and the gallant crew
  Will now die, as they lived, by each other.

Ah, sharp in his bosom meanwhile is the smart,
  He alone for his king is contending!
And the brightness and blaze of his youth in its prime
  Must here in mid-waves have its ending!

Unheeded the boat, for none care from their mates
  To steal off while the Prince is beside them;
And he will share all with his comrades true
  Till the death-plunge at last shall divide them.

The seas break over, the seas press in
  With a pale phosphoric streaming;
And a ripple runs over the vanishing deck,
  A blue cold witch-fire gleaming.

O then in a noble rebellion they rise;
  They may die, but the Prince shall o'erlive them!
With a loving rough force to the boat he is thrust,
  And he must be saved and forgive them!

Now their flame-pikes they lift, though the deck is one wave,
  Life's last light-signal above them:—
And each breast has one prayer for the mercy on high,
  And one for the far-off who love them.

O high-beating hearts that are still'd in the depths,
  Unknown treasure-caverns of Ocean!
There, where storms cannot vex, the three hundred are laid
  In their silent heroic devotion.

Rupert, nephew to Charles through his sister Elizabeth, wife to the Elector Palatine, after the ruin of his uncle's cause, carried on the struggle at sea. The incident here treated occurred on one of his last voyages, when cruising in the Atlantic near the Canaries: it is told at full length in E. Warburton's narrative of Rupert's life.

When he joined his uncle Rupert was only twenty-three years old; a fact which has been, apparently, ignored by the many civilian writers who have condemned him for the rashness and inconsiderate courage which he showed during the civil war, contrasting him with Fairfax or Cromwell as if he had been also a man of mature age. Ranke, as usual, treats him with more fairness.

Brother is parted from brother; Maurice, a year younger than himself,—then in the companion ship *Swallow*, in which Rupert, by the devoted determination of his comrades, was ultimately saved. Maurice was not long after drowned in the West Indies.

Flame-pikes: Two 'fire-pikes,' it is stated, were burned as a signal just before the flag-ship sank. Three hundred and thirty-three was the estimate of the number drowned.

DUNNOTTAR CASTLE

A Dirge

May : 1652

Dunnottar crag, Dunnottar crag,
The white waves round thee moan and fret;
Thy wind-worn tower and broken wall
With Freedom's nightly tears are wet.

Fair Freedom, in that struggle sore
When 'gainst the Southron Scotland stood,
This last asylum of the race
Was seal'd to thee by patriot blood.

In that long battle from the day
When ruthless Rome on Alban broke,
Or when the Wallace and the Bruce
Not idly smote 'gainst Edward's yoke,

Though Tweed's gray waters to the sea
With Flodden gore ennobled swept,—
The rock-wall'd fortress of the free,
The Lion-realm her freedom kept.

More precious than the Ophir mine
O holy Freedom! Virtue fair
May only put forth all her flowers
If nursed within thy liberal air!

The land so made herself; a race
Of stubborn energy and glow :—
Ah priceless birthright of the years!
Ah Liberty, at length laid low!

For Scotland's law and kirk and king,
'Gainst iron power, fanatic, coarse,
The unheavenly kingdom of the saints,
The peace imposed by despot force,

The deep uneasy lurid gloom
That atmosphered usurping sway,—
'Gainst these they fought, and died, and left
Their protest for a better day.

—Beyond the hills in burning blood
Flung o'er the far Atlantic wave,
With funeral flames the sun to-night
Has set upon a nation's grave.

A leaden cloud on hillside falls
And carse and loch and sea-ring'd shore :—

O long ere Freedom fair returns,
And Scotland is herself once more!

O moaning sea, O bitter storm,
Around Dunnottar rise and rave!
Fit requiem for a nation's fall,
Fit dirge for the forgotten brave!

Dunnottar Castle, situate on a rocky headland by Stonehaven in Kincardine, was the last place which stood out against Cromwell's forces when he invaded Scotland.

The position of the opposing powers in the Scotch campaign of 1650-1 is thus summarized by Ranke (xi: 3):—' Scotch Presbyteri-
' anism set itself once more in complete antagonism to the suprem-
' acy of the Independents, and to the Commonwealth in England.
' . . . Cromwell was recalled from Ireland . . . and placed as
' Lord-General at the head of the army which was to humble the
' Scots. It was now that Fairfax finally retired . . . He found
' himself in the unhappy position of a man who has allowed himself
' to be used as a tool.'

Lord Macaulay's summary of the campaign is in his best style.
' The ancient kingdom of the Stuarts was reduced, for the first
' time, to profound submission. Of that independence, so man-
' fully defended against the mightiest and ablest of the Planta-
' genets, no vestige was left. The English Parliament made law
' for Scotland. The English judges held assizes in Scotland.
' Even that stubborn Church, which has held its own against so
' many Governments, scarce dared to utter an audible murmur.'

THE RETURN OF LAW

1660

At last the long darkness of anarchy lifts, and the dawn
    o'er the gray
In rosy pulsation floods; the tremulous amber of day:
In the golden umbrage of spring-tide, the dewy delight
    of the sward,
The liquid voices awake, the new morn with music reward.
Peace in her car goes up; a rainbow curves for her road;
Law and fair Order before her, the reinless coursers of
    God;—
Round her the gracious maids in circling majesty shine;
They are rich in blossoms and blessings, the Hours, the
    white, the divine!
Hands in sisterly hands they unite, eye calling on eye;
Smiles more speaking than words, as the pageant sweeps
    o'er the sky.
Plenty is with them, and Commerce; all gifts of all lands
    from her horn
Raining on England profuse; and, clad in the beams of
    the morn,

Her warrior-guardian of old the red standard rears in its might;
And the Love-star trembles above, and passes, light into light.

Many the marvels of earth, the more wondrous wonders on high,
Worlds past number on worlds, blank lightless abysses of sky;
But thou art the wonder of wonders, O Man! Thy impalpable soul,
Atom of consciousness, measuring the Infinite, grasping the whole:
Then, on the trivialest transiencies fix'd, or plucking for fruit
Dead-sea apples and ashes of sin, more brute than the brute.
Yet in thy deepest depths, filth-wallowing orgies of night,
Lust remorseless of blood, yet, allow'd an inlet for light:
As where, a thousand fathom beneath us, midnight afar
Glooms in some well, and we gaze, and, behold! one flash of one star!
For, ever, the golden gates stand open, the transit is free
For the human to mix with divine; from himself to the Highest to flee.

Lo on its knees by the bedside the babe :—and the song
    that we hear
Has been heard already in Heaven! the low-lisp'd music
    is clear :—
For, fresh from the hand of the Maker, the child still
    breathes the light air
Of the House Angelic, the meadow where souls yet
    unbodied repair,
Lucid with love, translucent with bliss, and know not the
    doom
In the Marah valley of life laid up for the sons of the
    womb.
—I speak not of grovelling hearts, souls blind and
    begrimed from the birth,
But the spirits of nobler strain, the elect of the children
    of earth :—
For the needle swerves from the pole; they cannot do
    what they would;
In their truest aim is falsehood, and ill out-balancing
    good.
Faith's first felicities fade; the world-mists thicken and
    roll,
'Neath the heavens arching their heaven; o'er-hazing the
    eye of the soul.
Then the vision is pure no longer; refracted above us
    arise

The phantasmal figures of passion; earth's mirage exhaled to the skies.
And they go as the castled clouds o'er the verge when the tempest is laid,
Towering Ambition, and Glory, and Self as Duty array'd:—
Idols no less than that idol whom lustful Ammon of yore
With the death-scream of children, a furnace of blood, was fain to adore!
So these, in the shrine of the soul, for a Moloch sacrifice cry,
The conscience of candid childhood, the pure directness of eye:—
Till the man yields himself to himself, accepting his will as his fate,
And the light from above within him is darkness; the darkness how great!

O Land whom the Gods,—loving most,—most sorely in wisdom have tried,
England! since Time was Time, thrice swept by the conqueror tide,
Why on thyself thrice turn, thrice crimson thy greenness in gore,
With the slain of thy children, as sheep, thy meadows whitening-o'er?
Race impatiently patient; tenacious of foe as of friend;

Slow to take flame; but, enflamed, that burns thyself out
    to the end:
Slow to return to the balance, once moved; not easily
    sway'd
From the centre, and, star-like, retracing thy orbit through
    sunlight and shade!
—Without hate, without party affection, we now look
    back on the fray,
Through the mellowing magic of time the phantoms
    emerging to day!
Grasping too much for self, unjust to his rival in strife,
Each foe with good conscience and honour advances;
    war to the knife!
Lo, where with feebler hand the Stuart essays him to guide
The disdainful coursers of Henry, the Tudor car in its
    pride!
For he saw not the past was past; nor the swirl and inrush
    of the tide,
A nation arising in manhood; its will would no more be
    denied.
They would share in the labour and peril of State; they
    must perish or win;
'Tis the instinct of Freedom that cries; the voice of Nature
    within!
Narrow the cry and sectarian oft: true sons of their age;
Justice avenged unjustly; yet more in sorrow than rage;

Till they drank the poison of power, the Circé-cup of command,
And the face of Liberty fail'd, and the sword was snatch'd from her hand.
Now the scaffold-offerings blaze, and,—shame engendering shame,—
The hell-pack of war is laid close on the land for ruin and flame.
For as things most holy are worst, from holiness when they decline,
So Law, in the name of law once outraged, demon-divine,
Swoops back as Anarchy arm'd, and maddens her lovers of yore,
Changed from their former selves, baptized with the chrisom of gore.
Then Falkland and Hampden are gone; and darker counsels arise;
Vane with his tortuous soul, through over-wisdom unwise;
Pym, deep stately designer, the subtle in simple disguised,
Artist in plots, projector of panics he used, and despised!
—But as, in the mountain world, where the giants each lift up their horn
To the skies defiant and pale, and our littleness measure and scorn,
Frowning-out from their far-off summits: and eye and mind may not know

Which is hugest, where all are huge: But, as from the
    region we go
Receding, the Titan of Titans comes forth, and above
    him the sky
Is deepest: and lo!—'tis the White One, the Monarch!
    —He mounts, as we fly!
Or as over the sea the gay ships and dolphins glisten and
    flit,
And then that Leviathan comes, and takes his pastime
    in it;
And wherever he ploughs his dark road, they must sink
    or follow him still,
For his is the bulkiest strength, the proud and paramount
    will!
—Thou wast great, O King! (for we grudge not the style
    thou didst yearn-for in vain,
But a river of blood was between, and an ineffaceable
    stain),
Great with an earth-born greatness; a Titan of awe, not
    of love;
'Twas strength and subtlety balanced; the wisdom not
    from above.
For he leant o'er his own deep soul, oracular; over the
    pit
As the Pythia throned her of old, where the rock in
    Delphi was split;

And the vapour and echo within he mis-held for divine;
    and the land
Heard and obey'd, unwillingly willing, the voice of command.
—Soaring enormous soul, that to height o'er the highest
    aspires;
All that the man can seize being nought to what he desires!
And as, in a palace nurtured, the child to courtesy grows,
Becoming at last what it acts; so man on himself can
    impose,
Drill and accustom himself to humility, till, like an art,
The lesson the fingers have learn'd appears the command
    of the heart;
Whilst pride, as the snake of the juggler, obedient, curls
    in its place,
And he wears to himself and his fellows the mask that is
    almost a face.
Truest of hypocrites, he!—in himself entangled, he thinks
Earth uprising to Heaven, while earth-ward the heavenly
    sinks:
Conscience, we grant it, his guide; but conscience drugg'd
    and deceived;
Conscience which all that his self-belief whisper'd as
    Gospel believed.
And though he sought earnest for God, in life-long wrestle
    and prayer,

Yet the sky by a veil was darken'd, a phantom flitting in air;
For a cloud from that seething cavernous heart fumed out in his youth,
And whatever he will'd in the strength of the soul was imaged as truth :—
Grew with his growth : And now 'tis Ambition, disguised in success;
And he walks with the step assured, that cares not its issue to guess,
Clear in immediate purpose: and moulding his party at will,
He thrones it o'er obstinate sects, his ideal constrain'd to fulfil.
Cool in his very heat, self-master, he masters the realm :
God and his glory the flag; but King Oliver lord of the helm!
As he needs, steers crooked or straight; with his eye controlling the proud,
While blandness runs from his tongue, as the candidate fawns on the crowd;
Sagest of Titans, he stands; dark, ponderous, muddy-profound;
Greatness untemper'd, untuned; no song, but a chaos of sound :—
Yet the key-note is ever beneath : 'Mere humble instruments ! See!

'Poor weak saints, at the best: but who has triumph'd as we?'
Thanks the Lord for each massacre-mercy, his glory, for his is the Cause:
Catlike he bridles, and purrs about God: but within are the claws,
The lion-strength is within!—Vane, Ludlow, Hutchinson, knew,
When the bauble of Law disappear'd, and the sulky senate withdrew:
When the tyrannous Ten sword-silenced the land, and the necks of the strong
By the heel of their great Dictator were bruised, wrong trampling on wrong.
Least willing of despots! and fain the fair temple of Law to restore,
Sheathing the sword in the sceptre: But lo! as in legends of yore,
Once drawn, once redden'd, it may not return to the scabbard!—and straight
On that iron-track'd path he had framed to the end he is goaded by Fate.
And yet, as a temperate man, to flavour some exquisite dish,
Without stint pours forth the red wine, thus only can compass his wish;

Upon Erin the death-mark he brands, the Party and Cause to secure;
Not bloodthirsty by birth; just, liquor 'twas needful to pour;
Only the wine of man's blood! . . . But the horrible sacrament thrill'd
Right through the heart of a nation; nor yet is the memory still'd;
E'en yet the gray spectre returns, the ghost of the murderous years,
Blood yet flushing in hatred; and blood transmuted to tears!
—Ah strange drama of Fate! what motley pageantries rise
On the stage of this make-shift world! what irony silenced in sighs!
For as when the Swiss looks down on the dell, from the pass and the snow,
Sees the peace of the fields, the white farms, the clear equable streamlet below,
And before him the world unknown, the blaze of the shadowless Line,
Riches ill-purchased in exile, the toiling plantation and mine;
And the horn floats up the faint music of youth from his forefathers' fold,

And he sighs for the patient life, the peace more golden
 than gold :—
So He now looks back on the years, and groans 'neath the
 load he must bear,
Loving this England that loathed him, and none the
 burden to share!
Gagging not gaining souls: to the close he wonders in
 vain
Why he cannot win hearts: why 'tis only the will that
 resigns to his reign.
As that great image in Dura, the land perforce must obey,
Unloved, unlovely,—and not the feet only of iron and
 clay,—
Atlas of this wide realm! in himself he summ'd up the
 whole;
Its children the Cause had devour'd: the sword was
 childless and sole.

—Ah strange drama of Fate! what motley pageantries
 rise
On the stage of this make-shift world! what irony silenced
 in sighs!
For, as when the waves ebb in the strait beneath Etna,
 and Scylla betrays
The monster below, foul scales of the serpent and slime,
 —could we gaze

On Tyranny stript of her tinsel, what vision of dool and dismay !
Terror in confidence clothed, and anarchy biding her day:
Selfishness hero-mask'd; stage-tricks of the shabby-sublime;
Impotent gaspings at good; and the deluge after her time !

—Is it war that thunders o'er England, and bursts the millennial oak
From his base like a castle uprooted, and shears with impalpable stroke
The sails from the ocean, the houses of men, while the Conqueror lay
On the morn of his crowning mercy, and life flicker'd down with the day ?
Is it war on the earth, or war in the skies, or Nature who tolls
Her passing-bell as from earth they go up, her imperial souls ?
—He rests:—'Tis a lion-sleep: and the sternness of Truth is reproved:
The sleep of a leader of men; unhuman, to watch him unmoved !
In the stillness of pity and awe we remember his troublesome years,
For man is the magnet to man, and mortal failure has tears.

—He rests:—On the massive brows, as a rock by the
    sunrise is crown'd,
His passionate love for the land, in a glory-coronal bound!
And Mercy dawns fast o'er the dead, from the bier as we
    turn and depart,
England for England's sake clasp'd firm as a child to his
    heart.

—He rests:—And the storm-clouds have fled, and the
    sunshine of Nature repress'd
Breaks o'er the realm in smiles, and the land again has
    her rest.
He rests: the great spirit is hid where from heaven the
    veil is unroll'd,
And justice merges in love, and the dross is purged from
    the gold.

    The general point of view from which this subject is here approached is given in the following passages:—'The whole nation,' says Macaulay (1659), 'was sick of government by the sword, and 'pined for government by the law.' Hence, when Charles landed, 'the cliffs of Dover were covered by thousands of gazers, among 'whom scarcely one could be found who was not weeping with 'delight . . . Everywhere flags were flying, bells and music 'sounding, wine and ale flowing in rivers to the health of him 'whose return was the return of peace, of law, and of freedom.' Nor was this astonishing: the name of the Commonwealth, a greater than Macaulay remarks, 'was grown infinitely odious: it 'was associated with the tyranny of ten years, the selfish rapacity 'of the Rump, the hypocritical despotism of Cromwell, the arbi- 'trary sequestrations of committee-men, the iniquitous decimations 'of military prefects, the sale of British citizens for slavery in the

'West Indies, the blood of some shed on the scaffold without legal
'trial, . . . the persecution of the Anglican Church, the baccha-
'nalian rant of sectaries, the morose preciseness of puritans . . .
'It is universally acknowledged that no measure was ever more
'national, or has ever produced more testimonies of public appro-
'bation, than the restoration of Charles II . . . For the late
'government, whether under the parliament or the protector, had
'never obtained the sanction of popular consent, nor could have
'subsisted for a day without the support of the army. The King's
'return seemed to the people the harbinger of a real liberty, instead
'of that bastard Commonwealth which had insulted them with its
'name' (Hallam: *Const. Hist.* ch. x and xi).

Peace in her car: It will be seen that the Rospigliosi *Aurora*, Guido's one inspired work, has been here before the writer's memory.

On thyself thrice turn: The civil wars of the Barons, the Roses, and the Commonwealth.

He saw not: The secret of Charles's failure was that he, as Mr. Gardiner finely remarks, 'took counsel, as Bacon would have said, 'of the time past, not of the time present.' Ranke's dispassionate summary of the attempted 'arrest of five members,' which has been always held one of the King's most arbitrary steps, as it was, perhaps, the most fatal, illustrates this view: 'The prerogative of the 'Crown, *in the sense of the early kings*' (unconditional right of arrest, in cases of treason), 'and the privilege of Parliament, *in the sense of 'coming times*, were directly contradictory to each other': (viii : 10).

Till they drank the poison: A sentence weighty with his judicial force may be here quoted from Hallam :—' The desire of obtaining 'or retaining power, if it be ever sought as a means, is soon con-
'verted into an end.' The career of the Long Parliament supports this judgment: of it 'it may be said, I think, with not greater 'severity than truth, that scarce two or three public acts of justice, 'humanity, or generosity, and very few of political wisdom and 'courage, are recorded of them from their quarrel with the King to 'their expulsion by Cromwell': (*Const. Hist.* ch. x : Part i).

Artist in plots: See Ranke (viii : 5) for Pym's skilful use of a supposed plot, (the main element in which was known by himself to be untrue), in order to terrify the House and ensure the destruction of Strafford; and Hallam (ch. ix).—Admiration of Pym may be taken as a proof that a historian is ignorant of, or faithless to, the fundamental principles of the Constitution:—as the worship of Cromwell is decisive against any man's love of liberty, whatever his professions.

O King: 'Cromwell, like so many other usurpers, felt his posi-
' tion too precarious, or his vanity ungratified, without the name
' which mankind have agreed to worship.' The conversations recorded by Whitelock are conclusive on this point : 'and, though
' compelled to decline the crown, he undoubtedly did not lose sight
' of the object for the short remainder of his life' (*Hallam*).

Drill and accustom himself to humility : See Appendix.

The sky by a veil: See Appendix.

And he walks: 'He said on one occasion, *He goes furthest who knows not whither he is going*': (*Ranke :* xii : 1).

Purrs about God : Brilliant examples, (which at first sight might seem to justify a severer phrase), may be found by the curious in the frailties of poor human nature, *passim*, in Cromwell's "Letters and Speeches," accompanied by characteristic editorial comments, which are, however, of little use to those who seriously wish to comprehend and to do justice to Cromwell.

The tyrannous Ten : The Major-Generals, originally ten, (but the number varied), amongst whom, in 1655, the Commonwealth was divided. They displayed 'a rapacity and oppression beyond
' their master's' (*Hallam*) : a phrase amply supported by the hardly-impeachable evidence of Ludlow.

The horrible sacrament: See Appendix.

Why he cannot win hearts: 'In the ascent of this bold usurper
' to greatness ... he had encouraged the levellers and persecuted
' them ; he had flattered the Long Parliament and betrayed it ; he
' had made use of the sectaries to crush the Commonwealth ; he
' had spurned the sectaries in his last advance to power. These
' with the Royalists and Presbyterians, forming in effect the whole
' people ... were the perpetual, irreconcilable enemies of his
' administration' (*Hallam:* ch. x).

Stage tricks: See the curious regal imitations and adaptations of the Protector during his later years, in matters regarding his own and his family's titles and state, and the marriage of his daughters.

Mortal failure: See Appendix.

THE POET'S EUTHANASIA

November : 1674

CLOKED in gray threadbare poverty, and blind,
Age-weak, and desolate, and beloved of God ;
High-heartedness to long repulse resign'd,
Yet bating not one jot of hope, he trod
The sun and sky-less streets he could not see ;
By those faint feet made sacrosanct to me.

Yet on that laureate brow the sign he wore
Of Phoebus' wrath ; who,—for his favourite child,
When war and faction raised their rancorous roar,
Leagued with fanatic frenzy, blood-defiled,
To the sweet Muses and himself untrue,—
Around the head he loved thick darkness threw.

—He goes :—But with him glides the Pleiad throng
Of that imperial line, whom Phoebus owns
His ownest : for, since his, no later song
Has soar'd, as wide-wing'd, to the diadem'd thrones
That, in their inmost heaven, the Muses high
Set for the sons of immortality.

Most loved, most lovely, near him as he went,
Vergil: and He, supremest for all time,
In hoary blindness:—But the sweet lament
Of Lesbian love, the Parian song sublime,
Follow'd:—and that stern Florentine apart
Cowl'd himself dark in thought, within his heart

Nursing the dream of Church and Caesar's State,
Empire and Faith:—while Fancy's favourite child,
The myriad-minded, moving up sedate
Beckon'd his countryman, and inly smiled:—
Then that august Theophany paled from view,
To higher stars drawn up, and kingdoms new.

 The last ten years of Milton's life were passed in his house situate in the (then) 'Artillery Walk,' Bunhill, near Aldersgate. He is described as a spare figure, of middle stature or a little less, who walked, generally clothed in a gray camblet overcoat, in the streets between Bunhill and Little Britain.

 Phoebus' wrath: See Appendix.

 Since his: See Appendix.

 Vergil: placed first as most like Milton in consummate art and permanent exquisiteness of phrase. It is to him, also, (if to any one), that Milton is metrically indebted.—The other poets who are here classed as 'Imperial' are Homer, Sappho, Archilochus, Dante, Shakespeare.

 The dream: Dante's political wishes and speculations, wholly opposed to Milton's, are, however, like his in their impracticable originality.

 Theophany: Vision of the Gods.

WHITEHALL GALLERY

February 11 : 1685

As when the King of old
'Mid Babylonian gold,
And picture-woven walls, and lamps that gleam'd
Unholy radiance, sate,
And with some smooth slave-mate
Toy'd, and the wine laugh'd round, and music stream'd
Voluptuous undulation, o'er the hall,—
Till on the palace-wall

Forth came a hand divine
And wrote the judgment sign,
And Babylon fell:—So now, in that his place
Of Tudor-Stuart pride,
The golden gallery wide,
'Mid venal beauty's lavish-arm'd embrace,
And hills of gambler-gold, a godless King
Moved through the revelling

With quick brown falcon-eye
And lips of gay reply;

Wise in the wisdom not from Heaven!—as one
      Who from his exile-days
      Had learn'd to scorn the praise
Of truth, the crown by martyr-virtue won:
Below ambition:—Grant him regal ease!
      The rest, as fate may please!

      —O royal heir, restored
      Not by the bitter sword,
But when the heart of these great realms in free,
      Full, triple, unison beat
      The Victim's son to greet,
Her ancient law and faith and flag with thee
Rethroned,—not thus!—in this inglorious hall
      Of harem-festival,

      Not thus!—For even now,
      The blaze is on thy brow
Scored by the shadowy hand of him whose wing
      Knows neither haste nor rest;
      Who from the board each guest
In season calling,—knight and kerne and king,—
Where Arthur lies, and Alfred, signs the way;—
      —We know him, and obey.

Lord Macaulay's lively description of this scene (*Hist.* Ch. iv) should be referred to. 'Even then,' he says, 'the King had com-'plained that he did not feel well.'

Tudor-Stuart: This famous Gallery was of sixteenth-century date.

When the heart: 'The whole nation,' says Lord Macaulay, (ch. i), 'was sick of government by the sword, and pined for govern-'ment by the Law.'

'The Restoration,' says Professor Seeley, in an able essay on current perversions of seventeenth-century-history, 'was not a return 'to servitude, but the precise contrary. It was a great emancipa-'tion, an exodus out of servitude into liberty . . . As to the later 'Stuarts, I regard them as pupils of Cromwell: . . it was their 'great ambition to appropriate his methods,' (and, we may add, to follow his foreign policy in regard to France and Holland), 'for 'the benefit of the old monarchy. They failed where their model 'had succeeded, and the distinction of having enslaved England re-'mained peculiar to Cromwell.'

THE BALLAD OF KING MONMOUTH

1685

Fear not, my child, though the days be dark,
  Never fear, he will come again,
With the long brown hair, and the banner blue,
  King Monmouth and all his men!

  The summer-smiling bay
  Has doff'd its vernal gray;
A peacock breast of emerald shot with blue:
  Is it peace or war that lands
  On these gray quiet sands,
As round the pier the boats run-in their silent crew?

  Bent knee, and forehead bare;
  That moment was for prayer!
Then swords leap out, and—Monmouth!—is the cry:
  The crumbling cliff o'erpast,
  The hazard-die is cast,
'Tis James 'gainst James in arms! Soho! and Liberty!

—Fear not, my child, though he come with few;
   Alone will he come again;
God with him, and his right hand more strong
   Than a thousand thousand men!

    They file by Colway now;
    They rise o'er Uplyme brow;
And faithful Taunton hails her hero-knight:
    And girlhood's agile hand
    Weaves for the patriot band
The crown-emblazon'd flag, their gathering-star of fight.

    —Ah flag of shame and woe!
    For not by these who go,
Scythe-men and club-men, foot and hunger-worn,
    These levies raw and rude,
    Can England be subdued,
Or that ancestral throne from its foundations torn!

    Yet by the dour deep trench
    Their mettle did not blench,
When mist and midnight closed o'er sad Sedgemoor;
    Though on those hearts of oak
    The tall cuirassiers broke,
And Afric's tiger-bands spring out with sullen roar:

Though the loud cannon plane
Death's lightning-riven lane,
Levelling that unskill'd valour, rude, unled:
—Yet happier in their fate
Than whom the war-fiends wait
To rend them limb from limb, the gibbet-withering dead!

— Yet weep not, my child, though the dead be dead,
And the wounded rise not again !
For they are with God who for England fought,
And they bore them as Englishmen.

Stout hearts, and sorely tried!
—But he, for whom they died,
Skulk'd like the wolf in Cranbourne, gray and gaunt :—
Till, dragg'd and bound, he knelt
To one no prayers could melt,
Nor bond of blood, nor fear of fate, from vengeance daunt.

—O hill of death and gore,
Fast by the tower'd shore,
What wealth of precious blood is thine, what tears!
What calmly fronted scorn;
What pain, not vainly borne!
For heart beats hot with heart, and human grief endears!

—Then weep not, my child, though the days be dark ;
Fear not ; He will come again,
With Arthur and Harold and good Saint George,
King Monmouth and all his men !

Monmouth's invasion forms one of the most brilliant,—perhaps the most brilliant,—of Lord Macaulay's narratives. But many curious details are added in the History by Mr. G. Roberts (1844).

The belief, which this poem represents, that 'King Monmouth,' as he was called in the West, would return, lasted long. He landed in Lyme Bay, 11 June, 1685, between the Cobb and the beginning of the Ware cliffs : marching North, after a few days, by the road which left the ruins of Colway House on the right and led over Uplyme to Axminster.

Soho: the word on Monmouth's side at Sedgemoor; his London house was in the Fields, (now Square), bearing that name.

Faithful Taunton : here the Puritan spirit was strong ; and here Monmouth was persuaded to take the title of king (20 June), symbolized by the flag which the young girls of Taunton presented to him. It bore a crown with the cypher J.R. : Monmouth's own name being James.

Dark deep trench: Sedgemoor lies in a marshy district near Bridgewater, much intersected by trenches or 'Rhines.' One, the Bussex Rhine, lay between the two armies as they fought; 6 July. Monmouth was caught hiding in Cranbourne Chase, 8 July; executed, after a vain attempt to move the heart of his uncle the king, 15 July, on Tower Hill.

Afric's tiger-bands : Kirke's savage troops from Tangier.

WILLELMUS VAN NASSAU

YES! we confess it! 'mong the sons of Fate,
    Earth's great ones, thou art great!
As that tall peak which from her silver cone
    Of maiden snow unstain'd
All but the bravest scares, and bides alone

In glacier isolation: Thus wert thou,
    With that pale steadfast brow,
Gaunt-aquiline: Thy whole life one labouring breath;
    Yet the strong soul untamed;
France bridled, England saved, thy task ere death!

—O day of triumph, when thy bloodless host
    From Devon's russet coast
Through the fair capital of the garden-West,
    And that, whose gracious spire
Like childhood's prayer springs heaven-ward unrepress'd,

To Thames march'd legion-like; and at their tread
   The sullen despot fled,
And Law and Freedom fair,—so late restored,
   And to so-perilous life,
While Stuart craft replaced the Usurper's sword,—

Broke forth, as sunshine from the breaking sky,
   When vernal storm-wings fly!
That day was thine, great Chief, from sea to sea:
   The whole land's welcome seem'd
The welcome of one man! a realm by thee

Deliver'd!—But the crowning hour of fame,
   The zenith of a name
Is ours once only: and he, too just, too stern,
   Too little Englishman,
A nation's gratitude did not care to earn,

On wider aims, not worthier, set :—A soul
   Immured in self-control;
Saving the thankless in their own despite :—
   Then turning with a gasp
Of joy, to his own land by native right;

Changing the Hall of Rufus and the Keep
Of Windsor's terraced steep
For Guelderland horizons, silvery-blue;
The green deer-twinkling glades,
And long, long, avenues of the stately Loo.

'William,' says his great panegyrist, 'never became an English-
'man. He served England, it is true; but he never loved her,
'and he never obtained her love. To him she was always a land
'of exile, visited with reluctance and quitted with delight. . . .
'Her welfare was not his chief object. Whatever patriotic feeling
'he had was for Holland. . . . In the gallery of Whitehall he
'pined for the familiar House in the Wood at the Hague, and
'never was so happy as when he could quit the magnificence of
'Windsor for his humbler seat at Loo:' (*Macaulay: Hist.* ch. vii).

One labouring breath: William throughout life was tortured by asthma.

Devon's russet coast: Torbay.

Capital of the garden-West: Exeter.

Gracious spire: Salisbury.

Hall of Rufus: The one originally built by William II at Westminster.

A DIRGE OF REPENTANCE

October 1 : 1691

Who is she that cometh, in garments torn and forlorn,
    Tear-fray'd eyelids, a song that ceases in sighs,
Like a ghost that flits at the death-gasp hour of morn,
    And wails at the casement the child of the house, as he dies?
        Is it our sister from over sea?
        So worn, so mishandled, should it be she?
In the day of our night on her face the tokens of heaven were fair,
Where now is the blanching of sorrow, the gleam of the drops of despair.

The world she taught in the days of her mystic prime,
    And her light was a gracious light; the smile of a maid:
But she miss'd the stern lessons of Rome: she learn'd not in time
    The many-hued strands of the race in one kingdom to braid.
        As some bird in her wildwood golden and gay,
        To the northern ravening ravens a prey,

Through the limbs of the quivering land black Lurdane and Norman in hosts
Strike talons of steel, and, whole centuries, Harpy-like, flap round her coasts.

Ravenous they tear out the life of the land as they go;
　Tear up the old heart-marks of Erin, the culture and song;
Barbarized colonists match'd with a barbarous foe;
　Building a ruin on ruin, wrong buttressing wrong :—
　　For the perilous draught of absolute might
　　Maddens the good, in their own despite!
And the lust of a dominant race o'er the soil must lord it alone,
And the babe of an alien blood to the hounds, like vermin, is thrown.

Weak man is o'erpower'd by power: the tool in his hand
　Masters it; felling the tree he should shape and restrain;
Exterminates, where he should civilize; Levelling the land
　To a vacancy-peace, a Saharan verdureless plain:
　　And the Human dies from his heart in the day
　　When conscience and wish are uncheck'd in their sway;
Till the fiat of his own will seems divine, beyond his control;
And the Moloch of greed and of creed is set up as God in the soul.

Then horrors on horrors go by in demoniac dance:
  Babes steel-carved from the womb; and children that feast
On a mother's corpse; or toss'd by the jerk of the lance;
  The Image in man effaced, famish'd down to the beast:
    Barnsful of living fuel aglow;
    Caves, where a village stifles below;
Till death is stamp'd out by death, and silence and solitude reign,
And e'en the gray scavenger wolf thins off from the charnel-house plain.

—Yet they pass, they consume themselves, these horrors of blood!
  To his hut the peasant crawls, and the cradle once more
Smiles with delight, and the race comes back like a flood :—
  Then despot-dominance draws from its ruthless store
    A subtler torment, a keener knife;
    Touching the nerve of the land to the life,—
The old faith of that island of Saints, her heart's one comfort and stay,
Sole shelter of stricken souls, as they cower in tyranny's day.

Though the cross by the shrine with penitent kisses worn
    Be ground into highway dust, and the healing well
Choked; the bright-blazon'd pages of beauty torn
      From the holy books, the treasures of church and of cell:
        Though babes snatch'd off 'mid a Rachel-cry
        Be tortured the faith of the font to deny:—
O yet the warm heart of the race to its martyr-altars was true,
And clearer the passionate flame, as the storm with more bitterness blew!

—Gray hills, green meadows, rock-wall that re-echoes the dirge
    Of eternal Atlantic war, blow heavy on blow;
Clear and Kenmare, or where Achil whitens the surge
      Foaming it backward, a thousand torrents of snow!—
        Blue lakes that in chasms of greenery lie,
        Each inlaying on earth its own region of sky,
Mirrors of Nature!—made smooth to redouble her greatness and grace:
Not the gore-red and flame-red horizon of race death-wrestling with race!—

Inisfail! Fair sister! No sister was Albion to thee
    Through the Mid-Age days, nor when Tudor and Stuart had sway;

Stern Mountjoy, stern Strafford, and,—Caesar-Attila,—he
    Zealot and despot at once, with his iron array :—
        Or who, coldly great, when the war-tide had turn'd,
        Broke the pledges of freedom at Limerick earn'd,
Unjust to his better self:—O record of shame and of pain!
We scan thee with idle tears, sighs seeking atonement, in
        vain !

Justice Eternal! beholding the worlds from thy throne,
    Atoms that swim in the presence no creature can see,—
We have sinn'd! we have sinn'd! But remorse e'en yet
        may atone;
    A place for repentance is left, if we seek it in thee!
    We have sinn'd! we kneel with suppliant hand :
    O sisterly heart of a sister-land,
When the dawn is once more on thy hills, the star of thy
        bitterness set,
Forgiving the wrongs we confess,—the woes we remember,
        —forget !

    The date prefixed to this piece is the day when, by the signature of the treaty of Limerick, Ireland might have reasonably expected that England, freed by William III from religious persecution, would have, henceforth, governed her upon the lines of freedom and toleration. So far from this, says an eminently liberal and impartial writer, who has thrown much light on the 'dark places' of our history, 'The penal laws were the immediate consequence of ' the Revolution, and were mainly the work of the Whig party ;' quoting the magnificent words of Burke : 'All the penal laws of ' that unparalleled code of oppression were manifestly the effects of ' national hatred and scorn towards a conquered people, whom the ' victors delighted to trample upon, and were not at all afraid to ' provoke. *They were not the effect of their fears, but of their ' security:*' (*Lecky : History of England in the Eighteenth Century*, ch. ii).

In the day of our night: This and the following lines refer to the early civilization of Ireland, with which the names of Patrick and Columba are associated.

Maddens the good: See the treatment which even Edmund Spenser prescribes for Ireland under Elizabeth.

Then horrors on horrors: See Appendix.

Though the cross: Stringent laws were passed to suppress pilgrimages, and crosses and shrines of popular resort were savagely destroyed.

Pages of beauty: The extraordinary skill of the early Irish artists in illumination of manuscripts is well known.

Babes snatch'd off: See Appendix.

Caesar-Attila: See Appendix.

Broke the pledges of freedom: See Appendix.

THE CHILDLESS MOTHER

1700-1702

OFT in midnight visions
    Ghostly by my bed
Stands a Father's image,
    Gray discrownéd head :—
—I forsook thee, Father !
    Was no child to thee !
Child-forsaken Mother,
    Now 'tis so with me.

Oft I see the brother,
    Baby born to woe,
Crouching by the church-wall
    From the bloodhound-foe.
Evil crown'd of evil,
    Heritage of strife !
Mine, an heirless sceptre :
    His, an exile life !

—O my vanish'd darlings,
    From the cradle torn!
Dewdrop lives, that never
    Saw their second morn!
Buds that fell untimely,—
    Till one blossom grew;
As I watch'd its beauty,
    Fading whilst it blew.

Thou wert more to me, Love,
    More than words can tell:
All my remnant sunshine
    Went in one farewell.
Midnight-mirk before me
    Now my life goes by,
For the baby faces
    As in vain I cry.

O the little footsteps
    On the nursery floor!
Lispings light and laughter
    I shall hear no more!
Eyes that gleam'd at waking
    Through their silken bars;
Starlike eyes of children,
    Now beyond the stars!

Where the murder'd Mary
  Waits the rising sign,
They are laid in darkness,
  Little lambs of mine.
Only this can comfort :
  Safe from earthly harms
Christ the Saviour holds them
  In his loving arms :—

Spring eternal round him,
  Roses ever fair :—
Will his mercy set them
  All beside me there?
Will their Angels guide me
  Through the golden gate?
—Wait a little, children!
  Mother, too, must wait!

.

I forsook thee: Marlborough, desirous to widen the breach between Anne and William III, influenced her to write to her Father, ' supplicating his forgiveness, and professing repentance for the ' part she had taken.'

Now 'tis so: Anne 'was said to attribute the death of her children ' to the part she had taken in dethroning her father :' (*Lecky*).

The brother: The infant son of James, known afterwards as the 'Old Pretender,' or as James III. He was carried as an infant from the Palace (Dec. 1688) to Lambeth, where he was in great peril of discovery. The story is picturesquely told by Macaulay. Except for one brief and unfortunate time in Scotland, (1715), this prince is not known to have revisited his father's kingdom.

One blossom: The Duke of Gloucester, who grew up to eleven years, dying in July 1700. After his death Anne signed, in private letters, 'your unfortunate' friend.

Anne's character, says the candid Lecky, 'though somewhat 'peevish and very obstinate, was pure, generous, simple, and 'affectionate; and she displayed, under bereavements far more 'numerous than fall to the share of most, a touching piety that 'endeared her to her people.'

Where the murder'd Mary: 'Above and around, in every direc-'tion,' says Dean Stanley, describing the vault beneath the monument of Mary of Scotland in Henry the Seventh's Chapel,—'crushing 'by the accumulated weight of their small coffins the receptacles of 'the illustrious dust beneath, lie the eighteen children of Queen 'Anne, dying in infancy or stillborn, ending with William Duke 'of Gloucester, the last hope of the race:' (*Historical Memorials of Westminster Abbey*, ch. iii).

BLENHEIM

August 13 : 1704

OFT hast thou acted thy part,
My country, worthily thee !
Lifted up often thy load
Atlantean, enormous, with glee :—
For on thee the burden is laid to uphold
World-justice; to keep the balance of states;
On thee the long cry of the tyrant-oppress'd,
The oppress'd in the name of liberty, waits :—
Ready, aye ready, the blade
In its day to draw forth, unafraid;
Thou dost not blench from thy fate !
By the high heart, only, secure; by magnanimity, great.

E'en so it was on the morn
When France with Spain, in one realm
Welded, one thunderbolt, stood,
With one stroke the world to o'erwhelm.

—They have pass'd the great stream, they have stretch'd their white camp
Above the protecting morass and the dell,
Blenheim to Lutzingen, where the long wood
In summer-thick leafage rounds o'er the fell:
—England! in nine-fold advance
Cast thy red flood upon France;
Over marsh over beck ye must go,
Wholly together! or, Danube to Rhine, all slides to the foe!

As the lava thrusts onward its wall,
One mass down the valley they tramp;
Fascine-fill the marsh and the stream;
Like hornets they swarm up the ramp,
Lancing a breach through the long palisade,
Where the rival swarms of the stubborn foe,
While the sun goes high and goes down o'er the fight,
Sting them back, blow answering blow :—
O life-blood lavish as rain
On war's red Aceldama plain!
While the volleying death-rattle rings,
And the peasant pays for the pride and the fury-ambition of kings!

And as those of Achaia and Troia
By the camp on the sand, so they

In the aether-amber of evening
Kept even score in the fray;
Rank against rank, man match'd with man,
In backward, forward, struggle enlaced,
Grappled and moor'd to the ground where they stood,
As wrestlers wrestling, as lovers embraced :—
And the lightnings insatiable fly,
As the lull of the tempest is nigh,
And each host in its agony reels,
And the musket falls hot from the hand, enflamed by the death that it deals.

But as when through the vale the rain-clouds
Darker and heavier flow,
Above them the dominant summit
Stands clad in calmness and snow;
So thou, great Chief, awaiting the turn
Of the purple tide :—And the moment has come!
And the signal-word flies out with a smile,
And they charge the foe in his fastness, home :—
As one long wave when the wind
Urges an ocean behind,
One line, they sweep on the foe,
And France from our battle recoils, and Victory edges the blow.

As a rock by blue lightning divided
Down the hillside scatters its course,
So in twain their army is parted
By the sabres sabring in force:
They have striven enough for honour! . . and now
Crumble and shatter, and sheer o'er the bank
Where torrent Danube hisses and swirls
Slant and hurry in rankless rank :—
    There are sixty thousand the morn
    'Gainst the Lions marching in scorn;
    But twenty, when even is here,
Broken and brave and at bay, the Lilied banner uprear.

—So be it!—All honour to him
Who snatch'd the world, in his day,
From an overmastering King,
A colossal imperial sway!
Calm adamantine endurant chief,
Fit forerunner of him, whose crowning stroke,
Rousing his Guards on the Flandrian plain,
Unvassall'd Europe from despot yoke!
    He who from Ganges to Rhine
    Traced o'er the world his red line
    Irresistible; while in the breast
Reign'd devotedness utter, and self for England suppress'd!

O names that enhearten the soul,
Blenheim and Waterloo!
In no vain worship of glory
The poet turns him to you!
O sung by worthier song than mine,
If the day of a nation's weakness rise,
Of the little counsels that dare not dare,
Of a land that no more on herself relies,—
O breath of the great ones that were,
Burn out this taint in the air!
The old heart of England restore,
Till the blood of the heroes awake, and cry in her bosom
once more!

—Morning is fresh on the field
Where the war-sick champions lie,
By the wreckage of stiffening dead,
The anguish that yearns but to die.
Ah note of human agony heard
The paean of victory over and through!
Ah voice of duty and justice stern
That, at e'en this price, commands them to do!
And a vision of glory goes by,
Veil'd head and remorseful eye,
A triumph of death!—And they cried
'Only less dark than defeat is the morning of conquest';
—and sigh'd.

R

Blenheim is fully described in Lord Stanhope's *Reign of Queen Anne*. Its importance as a critical battle in European history lies in the fact that the work of the Great Alliance against the paramount power of France under Lewis XIV, (which England had unwisely fostered from Cromwell to James II), was secured by this victory. 'The loss of France could not be measured by men or 'fortresses. A hundred victories since Rocroi had taught the 'world to regard the armies of Lewis as all but invincible, when 'Blenheim and the surrender of the flower of the French soldiery 'broke the spell': (Green: *History of the English People:* B. VIII: ch. iii).

'The French and Bavarians, who numbered, like their opponents, 'some fifty thousand men, lay behind a little stream which ran 'through swampy ground to the Danube. . . . . It was not till 'midday that Eugene, who commanded on the right, succeeded in 'crossing the stream. The English foot at once forded it on the 'left.' They were repelled for the time. But, in the centre, Marlborough, 'by making an artificial road across the morass which 'covered it,' in two desperate charges turned the day.

A map of 1705 in the *Annals of Queen Anne's Reign*, shows vast hillsides to the right of the Allies covered with wood. This map also specifies the advance of the English in nine columns.

Only less: 'Marlborough,' says Lord Stanhope, 'was a humane 'and compassionate man. Even in the eagerness to pursue fresh 'conquests he did not ever neglect the care of the wounded.'

AT HURSLEY IN MARDEN

1712

We count him wise,
Timoleon, who in Syracuse laid down
    That gleaming bait of all men's eyes,
And for his cottage changed the invidious crown;
Moving serenely through his grayhair'd day
        'Mid vines and olives gray.

He also, whom
The load of double empire, half the world
    His own, within a living tomb
Press'd down at Yuste,—Spain's great banner furl'd
The winding-sheet around him,—while he strove
        The impalpable Above,

Though mortal yet,
To breathe, is blazon'd on the sages' roll:—
    High soaring hearts, who could forget
The sceptre, to the hermitage of the soul
Retired, sweet solitudes of the musing eye,
        And let the world go by!

There, if the cup
Of Time, that brims ere we can reach repose,
　　Fill'd slow, the soul might summon up
The strenuous heat of youth, the silenced foes;
The deeds of fame, star-bright above the throne;
　　　　The better deeds unknown.

There, when the cloud
Eased its dark breast in thunder, and the light
　　Ran forth, their hearts recall the loud
Hoarse onset roar, the flashing of the fight;
Those other clouds piled-up in white array
　　　　Whence deadlier lightnings play.

There, when the seas
Murmur at midnight, and the dome is clear,
　　And from their seats in heaven the breeze
Loosens the stars, to blaze and disappear,
And such is Glory! . . . with a sigh suppress'd
　　　　They smile, and turn to rest.

—But he, who here
Unglorious hides, untrain'd, unwilling Lord,
　　The phantom king of half a year,
From England's throne push'd by the bloodless sword,
Unheirlike heir to that colossal fame;—
　　　　How should men name his name,

How rate his worth
With those heroic ones who, life's labour done,
   Mark'd out their six-foot couch of earth,
The laurell'd rest of manhood's battle won?
—Not so with him! . . . Yet, ere we turn away,
     A still small voice will say,

     By other rule
Than man's coarse glory-test does God bestow
   His crowns: exalting oft the fool,
So deem'd, and the world-hero levelling low.
—And he, who from the palace pass'd obscure,
     And honourably poor,

     Spurning a throne
Held by blood-tenure, 'gainst a nation's will;
   Lived on his narrow fields alone,
Content life's common service to fulfil;
Not careful of a carnage-bought renown,
     Or that precarious crown:—

     Him count we wise,
Him also! though the chorus of the throng
   Be silent: though no pillar rise
In slavish adulation of the strong:—
But here, from blame of tongues and fame aloof,
     'Neath a low chancel roof,

—The peace of God,—
He sleeps: unconscious hero! Lowly grave
  By village-footsteps daily trod
Unconscious: or while silence holds the nave,
And the bold robin comes, when day is dim,
  And pipes his heedless hymn.

Timoleon: was invited from Corinth by the Syracusans (B.C. 344) to be their leader in throwing off the tyranny of the second Dionysius. Having effected this, defeated the Carthaginian invaders, and reduced all the minor despotisms within Sicily, he voluntarily resigned his paramount power and died in honoured retirement.

He also: In 1556 the Emperor Charles V gave up all his dominions, withdrawing in 1557 to Yuste;—a monastery situated in a region of singular natural beauty, between Xarandilla and Plasencia in Estremadura. He died there, Sept. 21, 1558; 'For some 'moments,' says Stirling, 'he silently contemplated the figure of 'the Saviour, and then clasped the crucifix to his bosom. Those 'who stood nearest to the bed now heard him say quickly, as if 'replying to a call, *Ya, voy, Senor,*—Now, Lord, I go:' (*Cloister Life of the Emperor Charles the Fifth*).

The phantom king: Richard Cromwell was Protector from Sept. 3, 1658 to May 25, 1659. After 1660 his life was that of a simple country gentleman, till his death in 1712, when he was buried at Hursley near Winchester.

Unheirlike heir: See Appendix.

THE TOWER OF DOOM

June 20: 1756

O NIGHT, one night, that work'd the work of years!
Plough'd the fair flesh, and smote the gold to gray;
Transmuting youth with age, 'twixt eve and day;
    Searing the fount of tears

In that hell-heat, and hoarsening the cry
Of those who watch'd the Ganges-brimming jars
In fiendish mock borne past their dungeon bars,
    Upheld unreachably nigh,

While tawny faces laugh'd with horrid gleam,
As eyes that laugh and glare in tiger-spite,
Seen of the traveller by sad lightning light,
    Through the thick jungle steam.

Ah, shrieks and heads that toss'd and fought for air,
As toward the shore their arms when swimmers throw!
Hands grasp'd in tearless glance of final woe!
    And voice of patient prayer

Calm in that chaos :—Rage, and fear, and faith,
Pent face to face ! Our mortal nature tried
Through all its diapason, deep and wide !
    —Then, the dense hush of death.

As on the braeside when the gorse is dry
In autumn, and men come to burn the hill,
And through the gorse the white flame leaps at will,
    And the strong branches cry

And start and thraw in that fierce furnace-flare :
When lo ! the fires are spent ; the smoke-wreaths cease,
And the tall stems in leafless lifeless peace
    Blacken the braeside bare :—

So they, those hundred Englishmen, and more,
Charr'd without flame, and smouldering till the day !
—O victims of tyrannic brutal play,
    Like them whose later gore

Stain'd the black well of horror, in the grove
Of gay Cawnpore, beneath the unpitying sun,
Babe mix'd with mother, one in death, as one
    Before in life and love :—

O victims! on your grave the throne is set
Of that great rule from sea to sea outspread,
Himalah to Taprobané!—But the dead
   Call on us to forget

Their transient wrongs; with lenient hand unite
The broken brotherhood of God's human-kind;
And in one realm the Kingdom-Empire bind
   Of Law, and Peace, and Right.

Lord Mahon tells vividly, (*History:* ch. xl), the sad and familiar story of the 'Black Hole' in the fort of Calcutta.

The Ganges-brimming jars: Water was brought at one time to the window, but could not be introduced through the bars. The guards mocked the vain struggles of their prisoners, holding up lights 'with fiendish glee.'

Those hundred . . . and more: of 146 who, on the evening before, had entered the prison, only 23 came forth.

Brutal play: The massacre appears to have been neither planned nor regretted by Surajah Dowlah.

The throne is set: The fate of India was implicity decided at Plassey, fought (June 23, 1757) as the final result of the Calcutta tragedy.

Taprobané: ancient name of Ceylon.

WOLFE AT QUEBEC

September 13 : 1759

Now the boat with her warrior-load glides off from the shore
  In a muffled stillness the silver surface to skim,
As the wild swans row their way with invisible oar,
  Breasting a glassy ripple while onward they swim :—
    In a stillness of midnight they go ;
    And it blazes above them, below ;
For the dome with the lamps of God is hung, and beneath on the brine
O'er the sea-ward current each star lays out his tremulous line.

On the left, where the galaxy whitens, the Bear to the north
  Points, the ramparting rocks their darkness uprear ;
Crested and jagg'd, while the fir stands sentinel forth,
  And the maple climbs in its beauty, ruddily sere :
    And the silence of Nature and night
    Strikes them with fearless affright ;

For mass'd on the precipice-rampart, unscaleable, o'er
    them they know
With his thousands the gallant Montcalm in calmness
    biding his blow.

—Ah! little they know, that midnight, each side, what
    the day
  Brings forth, an equal award of glory and grief!
Eyes that ere night will be closed with the battle's red
    clay;
  Limbs to be gather'd and bound in death's purple-ear'd
    sheaf:
    For the dead on the mountain will lie
    As an altar lift up to the sky;
And the triumph is downcast and veil'd, for the bulwarks
    of battle are low,
And the death-crown wreathed for the victor enwreathes
    the bier of the foe!

—But they slide with the sliding stream, and the stars in
    their height
  Aid: and the soul of our chief burns in him . . 'O
    Fame,
'Fame of duty accomplish'd, and pride of the fight,
  'Ye are great! But greater to me and purer thy
    name,

'Poet! subduing the heart
'With eternal exquisite art;
'Who in music givest thy soul, a sweetness softer than sighs;
'Holding earth bound in the strain that the spirit has learn'd in the skies!'

—Wolfe and Montcalm!—twin heroes in courage and death,
If he, our Simonides, sleep in the field of his song,
Yet the cry of your deeds, your high inviolate faith,
In the heart of men yet resounds, and bids them be strong!
For no faint foot may prevail
The mountain of manhood to scale :—
O Toil corroding the soul! alone thou touchest the height;
The crown of patriot virtue, the fame unfading and white!

While the fir: The precipice was overgrown with 'maple and 'spruce and ash trees.'

Greater to me: 'How intently,' says Lord Mahon, describing the attack on Quebec, 'must every eye have contemplated the dark 'outline as it lay pencilled upon the midnight sky,—and as every 'moment it grew closer and clearer,—of the hostile heights! Not 'a word was spoken, not a sound was heard beyond the rippling

' of the stream. Wolfe alone,—thus tradition has told us,—re-
' peated in a low voice to the other officers in his boat those beauti-
' ful stanzas with which a Country Church Yard inspired the muse
' of Gray. At the close Wolfe added, *Now, gentlemen, I would
' rather be the author of that poem, than take Quebec*': (*Mahon's
Hist.* ch. xxxv).

Wolfe's brilliant victory is also one of the most critical in our history. 'The destruction of the French power in America
' removed the one ever-pressing danger which secured the depend-
' ence of the English colonies on the mother-country. The great
' colonial forces raised . . . gave the colonies for the first time
' a consciousness of their strength, and furnished them with leaders
' for the War of Independence; while the burden of the debt due
' to the lavish expenditure of Pitt revived that scheme for the taxa-
' tion of America which led in a few years to the dismemberment
' of the Empire:' (Lecky: *England in the Eighteenth Century*: ch. viii).

Wolfe and Montcalm: A memorial at public cost was placed in Westminster Abbey to Wolfe. 'But the noblest monument to his
' memory is one that blends his fame with the fame of his gallant
' enemy,—far different, indeed, as to success, but alike both in
' courage and in doom. At Quebec now stands an obelisk, its
' front to the land-side, along which the French General moved,
' inscribed MONTCALM; its south front, towards which the English
' General advanced, bears the word WOLFE:' (*Mahon:* ch. xxxv).

Our Simonides: Gray died 30 July 1771, and was buried in the church-yard of Stoke near Slough:—The last lines of this stanza are founded upon a noble fragment by that great ancient lyrist to whom I have ventured to compare him.

JOHNSON AND THOSE ABOUT HIM:

The Club

1764

 VANDYCK of thine own age, and more!
 Great Master, thou, through visible art
 The inner man, the heart of heart,
God's image by world-handling varnish'd o'er,
  The soul enchased in fleshly shrine,
  To body forth in hue and line—

 Reynolds!—Thy century yet we see;
 Men, minds, and manners in the glass
 Thy genius holds to Nature pass,
Child, matron, warrior, snatch'd from death by thee:—
  Sweet chronicler! To thy name we pay
  The gratitude of a lesser day!

 To that fine skill a joy we owe
 For ever:—None more prized, than him,
 The face thy pencil loved to limn,
The vanish'd form known as ourselves we know,
  The friend whose image ne'er can fade,
  By love's own magic twice pourtray'd.

—Great son of Nature, born to years
Of unperceived and inner change
Slow drifting far beyond the range
Of thy strong youth! Thy name to us endears
The little city of thy birth
With equal thoughts of gloom and mirth.

For in that formal-featured day
Of dominant reason, on thy heart
The sorrow of the world, the smart
Of those who feel, the stress of mystery, lay:—
And then, as lightning clears the air,
Thy trenchant speech flash'd out, to bare

The sophistries of the worldly crowd;
The narrow bounds of life reveal'd,
The stumbling steps, the rugged field;
Yet how the twilight-rays to man allow'd
To reasoning souls unveil above
The sun of Theanthropic Love.

Yet not without his hour of strife
And hidden wrestling, truth-compell'd,
He wrought and reach'd the faith he held,
And fought the cruel daily fight of life:
Self-bow'd to labour and endure,
Broad-natured, scornful-silent, poor.

'Rude,' sneers the world; yet inly sound;
Subscribing *Dinnerless*, could plead
Acceptance for another's need;
Poor, and hence tender to the poor around:—
Impatient patience! Surly skin
Guarding the golden heart within!

The ragged sage I often see
Stoop to the ragged printer's knave,
Minerva's meanest awestruck slave,
Bettering advice with gold: Scene worthy thee
Unique Hogarth! whom first, alone,
Among our kings of art we throne.

Or in that homeless home, where blind
And sick and wormwood-temper'd strove
The gratitude of mankind to prove,
We watch that burly form, invincibly kind!
Or, as the din to warfare grew,
By Streatham's hearth his life renew.

Or how some street-sunk outcast thing,
By sin and scorn and famine cursed,
He bore with stalwart stride, and nursed,
Ignoring all her shame, and comforting;
And laugh'd a Titan laugh, to hear
How gossip wink'd with vacuous sneer.

—Across Time's jealous gulf appears
The court and senate where he ruled:
The light-soul'd bard by life unschool'd,
Yet in his very mirth a sound of tears;
'Mund's' Erin-eloquent eager eye,
And Langton's classic courtesy.

Then, o'er the silences, we hear
The bursts of sense and humour go;
The heaving frame, the home-thrust blow;
And bless the wisely-foolish chronicler,
Devoted heart, whose votive page
Paints and preserves that honour'd age!

Great 'mong the great ones of thy land,
Strange fate that bids thee thus, o'er all
The millions veil'd beyond recall,
Amongst us yet, in living presence, stand!
Our hidden heroes we revere;
But thou, as friend with friend, art here!

—Ah! well to see thee thus, when life
Was bright with fame and friendship won;
The peace of toil and duty done;
Unshadow'd by the fears of mortal strife;
The waning strength, the breathless breath,
And hard inclemency of death!

'The Club :' To this Society, founded in 1764 by Sir Joshua Reynolds and himself, Johnson owed hours which 'seemed to be 'the happiest of his life.' It gradually included a large proportion of the best men of an age fertile in eminence.

Great Master: The first gift of Reynolds as portraitist is that ' profound feeling for the indescribable thoughts of the inward ' man,' in which Wilkie the painter justly traced one of the points of resemblance between Sir Joshua and Michelangelo.

The little city of thy birth: Lichfield, where Johnson was born Sept. 18, 1709.

Subscribing Dinnerless : The famous letter to Mr. Cave, signed *Impransus*, (Sept. 1738), is followed by one in which Johnson recommends a 'humble labourer in literature,' perhaps even poorer than himself, for employment.

The printer's knave: See this characteristic scene, worthy also of Mulready or the elder Leslie, in Boswell, March 27, 1775. The other incidents to which allusion is made are, or should be, familiar to every self-respecting reader.

The senate where he ruled: Goldsmith, Burke, whose Christian name was affectionately shortened to *Mund*, Bennet Langton, are here specified :—but many others live for us in the pages of Boswell, an artist as unique in his style as Hogarth himself.

The waning strength : Johnson's manly courage and endurance of pain, contending with fear of death, during his last years, is one of the many pathetic pictures which we owe to the exquisite candour of Boswell's narrative.

CHARLES EDWARD AT ROME

1785

    O SUNSET, of the dawn
Unworthy!—that, so brave, so clear, so gay;
This, prison'd in low-hanging earth-mists gray,
    All grace and light withdrawn :—
Sad sunset of a royal race in gloom,
Accomplishing to the end the dolorous Stuart doom!

    Ghost of a king, he sate
In Rome, the city of ghosts and thrones outworn,
Drowsing his thoughts in wine ;—a life forlorn ;
    Pageant of faded state ;
Aged before old age, and all that past,
Like a forgotten thing of shame, behind him cast.

    Yet if by chance the cry
Of the sharp pibroch in his chamber thrill'd,
He felt the pang of high hope unfulfill'd :—
    And once, when one came by
With the dear name of Scotland on his lips,
The heart broke forth behind that forty-years' eclipse,

Triumphant in its pain :—
Then the old days of Holyrood halls return'd;
The leaden lethargy from his soul he spurn'd,
  And was the Prince again :—
All Scotland waking in him; all her bold
Chieftains and clans :—and all their tale, and his, he
    told:

—Told how, o'er the boisterous seas
 From faithless France he danced his way
 Where Alban's thousand islands lay,
The kelp-strown ridge of the lone Hebrides :—
How down each strath they stream'd as autumn rills,
  When he to Finnan vale
  Came from Glenaladale,
And that snow-handful grew an avalanche of the hills.

 There Lochiel, Glengarry there,
 Macdonald, Cameron : souls untried
 In war, but stout in mountain-pride
All odds against all worlds to laugh and dare :
Unpurchaseable faith of chief and clan!
  Enough! Their Prince has thrown
  Himself upon his own!
By hearts not heads they count, and manhood measures
    man!

—Torrent from Lochaber sprung,
Through Badenoch bare and Athole turn'd,
The fettering Forth o'erpast and spurn'd,
Then on the smiling South in fury flung;
Now gather head with all thine affluent force,
Draw forth the wild mellay!
At Preston is the fray;
Scotland 'gainst England match'd: White Rose against White Horse!

Cluster'd down the slope they go,
Red clumps of ragged valour, down,
While morn-mists yet the hill-top crown :—
Clan Colla! on !—the Camerons touch the foe!
One touch !—the battle breaks: the fight is fought,
As summit-boulders glide
Riddling the forest-side,
And in one moment's crash an army melts to nought!

—Ah gay nights of Holyrood!
Star-eyes of Scotland's fairest fair,
Sun-glintings of the golden hair,
Life's tide at full in that brief interlude!
Then as a bark slips from her natural coast
Deep into seas unknown,
Scotland went forth alone,
Unfriended, unallied; a handful 'gainst a host.

By the Border moorlands bare,
By faithless Solway's glistening sands,
And where Caer Luel's dungeon stands,
Gray keep of ancient Urien, huge, foursquare :—
Preston, and loyal Lancashire ; . . and then
From central Derby down,
To strike the royal town,
And to his German realm the usurper thrust again !

—O the lithesome mountaineers,
Wild hearts with royal boyhood high,
And victory in each forward eye,
While stainless honour his white banner rears !
Then all the air with mountain-music thrill'd,
The bonnets o'er the brow,—
My gallant clans ! . . . and now
The voices closed in earth, in death the pibroch still'd !

—As beneath Ben Aille's crest
The west wind builds its roof of gray,
And all the glory of the day
Blooms off from loch and copse and green hill-breast ;
So, when that fatal council spoke retreat,
The craven shameful word
They heard,—and scarcely heard !
And e'en at Scotland's name the blood refused to beat.

—O soul-piercing stroke of shame!
O last, last, chance,—and wasted so!
Work wanting but the final blow,—
And, then, the hopeless hope, the crownless name,
The heart's desire defeated!—What boots now
    That ice-brook-temper'd will,
    Indomitable still
As on through snow and storm their path the dalesmen plough?

—Yet again the tartans hail
One smile of Scotland's ancient face;
One favour waits the faithful race,—
One triumph more at Falkirk crowns the Gael!
And O! what drop of Scottish blood that runs
    Could aught, save do or die,
    And Bannockburn so nigh?
What cause to higher height could animate her sons?

    Up the gorse-embattled brae,
With equal eager feet they dash,
And on the moorland summit clash,
Friend mix'd with foe in stormy disarray:
Once more the Northern charge asserts its right,
    As with the driving rain
    They drive them down the plain:
That star alone before Drummossie gilds the night.

—Ah! No more!—let others tell
The agony of the mortal moor;
Death's silent sheepfold dotted o'er
With Scotland's best, sleet-shrouded as they fell!
There on the hearts, once mine, the snow-wreaths drift;
The winter dews at will
In bitter tears distil,
And o'er the field the stars their squadrons coldly shift.

Faithful in a faithless age!
Yet happier, in their death-dew drench'd,
In each rude hand the claymore clench'd,
Than who, to soothe a nation's craven rage,
To the red scaffold went with steady eye,
And the red martyr-grave,
For one, who could not save!
Who only lives to weep the weight of life, and die!

—He ended, with such grief
As fits and honours manhood:—Then, once more
Weaving that long romantic lay, told o'er
The names of clan and chief
Who perill'd all for him, and died;—and how
In islets, caves, and clefts, and bare high mountain-
brow

  The wanderer hid, and all
His Odyssey of woes!—Then, agonized
Not by the wrongs he suffer'd and despised,
  But for the Cause's fall,—
The faces, loved and lost, that for his sake
Were raven-torn and blanch'd, high on the traitor's stake,

  As on Drummossie drear
They fell,—as a dead body falls,—so he;
Swoon-senseless at that killing memory
  Seen across year on year:
O human tears! O honourable pain!
Pity unchill'd by age, and wounds that bleed again!

  —Ah, much enduring heart!
Ah soul, miscounsell'd oft and lured astray,
In that long life-despair, from wisdom's way
  And thy young hero-part!—
—And yet—DILEXIT MULTUM!—In that cry
Love's gentler judgment pleads; thine epitaph a sigh!

  The sad old age of Prince Charles is described by Lord Mahon [Stanhope] in his able *History:* ch. xxx: and some additional details will be found in Chambers' narrative of the expedition. During his later life, an almost entire silence seems to have been maintained by the Prince upon his earlier days and his royal claims. But the bagpipe was occasionally heard in the Roman Palace, and a casual visit, which Lord Mahon fixes in 1785, drew forth the recital which is the subject of this poem. The prince fainted as he recalled what his Highland followers had gone through, and his daughter rushing in exclaimed to the visitor, 'Sir! what is this! 'You must have been speaking to my father about Scotland and 'the Highlanders! No one dares to mention these subjects in his 'presence:' (*Mahon:* ch. xxvi).

Drowsing his thoughts: The habit of intemperance, common in that century to many who had not Charles Edward's excuses, appears to have been learned during the long privations which accompanied his wanderings, between Culloden and his escape to France.

Hebrides: Charles landed at Erisca, an islet between Barra and South Uist, in July 1745.

Fettering Forth: 'Forth,' according to the proverb, 'bridles the 'wild Highlandman.'—Charles passed it at the Ford of Frew, about eight miles above Stirling.

At Preston: Sept. 21, 1745.

White Horse: The armorial bearing of Hanover.

Clan Colla: general name for the sept of the Macdonalds.

Caer Luel: Urien ap Urbgen is an early hero of Strathclyde or Alcluith, the British kingdom lying between Dunbarton and Carlisle, then Caer Luel.

From central Derby: See Appendix.

Ben Aille: a mountain over Loch Ericht in the central Highlands.

Ice-brook-temper'd: 'It is a sword of Spain, the ice-brook's 'temper:' (*Othello:* A. 5 : S. 2).

At Falkirk: Jan. 17, 1746. 'On the eve after his victory 'Charles again encamped on Bannockburn.'

The mortal moor: named Culloden and Drummossie : Ap. 16, 1746. The cold at that time was very severe.

A nation's craven rage: See Appendix.

Love's gentler judgment: It is also pleasant to record that over the coffin of Charles in St. Peter's, Rome, a monument was placed by George the Fourth, on which, by a graceful and gallant 'act of 'oblivion,' are inscribed the names of James the Third, Charles the Third, and Henry the Ninth, 'Kings of England.'

SIMPLICITY:

Reynolds to his little Model Theophila

1789

GOLDEN head, that bears the sun
Wheresoe'er the feet may run;
Little feet, that hardly know
If on earth or air they go;
Lips through which the soul of glee
Lisps its gracious fancies free;
Eyes whose lucid depths confess
All the heart's ingenuousness;
Love unstinted, eager, pure;—
Womanhood in miniature;
—Ah! what wild rose sweet as this is,
Flower of love and many kisses?

On the grass, where flicker fair
Sunshafts of the summer air,
While the cuckoo's mellow note
Bell-like through the leaves may float,
Holding restless childhood's breast
For a moment charm'd to rest,—

Sit and turn thy head from me
In thy white simplicity;
While the golden ringlets streak
Shadows on the sunbright cheek,
And thy little hands fold up
Flowers in their flower-soft cup.

Sit thee there! Upon thy head
Silent shadows softly shed;
Whilst an inward light outflows
Round thee from the lips of rose,
Lips and limbs, by life beneath
Flush'd with youthful eager breath :—
As some fairy-bride array'd,
Inmate meet for woodland shade:
All thy baby form below
Shaped as if through gauzy snow;
Each line of the childly dress
Sharing childhood's sacredness.

Flower we name her: yet she best,
In her native sweet unrest,
In the smiled and hurried rush
Of the little words that gush,
Should be liken'd to the spring
That can only run and sing

To its inner own delight:
—Ah! . . We ne'er shall name her right!
Our rude speech cannot express
Childhood's utter tenderness!
She is framed of finer stuff:
Darling is not dear enough!

—Yet, if these alone were thine,
Warm soft limbs and features fine,—
We might pass and leave thee there
Lily-flower in woodland fair!
But already reason moves
On the candid lips she loves;
But already in the eye
Glancings of the soul we spy;
See the maiden heart within
Breathe out in the blushing skin;
On the stainless forehead trace
Lines of the immortal race.

True, fair Child!—These flower-like charms
All must vanish from our arms;
True, too true!—and thou must share
Buffets of life's ruder air.
But the eternal child within,
As this fair veil waxes thin,

As the faint feet downward go,
Loftier lineaments will show;
All transfused with perfect light
Radiated from Heaven's height;
Waiting till the voice of Love
That white purity calls above.

'Simplicity,' one of the most lovely of Reynolds' many lovely pictures of children, was exhibited in 1789, the year in which, at 66, his eyesight failed him. It was painted from Theophila Gwatkin, child of his favourite niece, born Theophila Palmer, and married in 1781.

As Sir W. Scott may be truly said to have created the Highland life in literature, so Sir J. Reynolds created childhood in art. There had been attempts, of course, before: but he was the first painter who felt and expressed the full beauty, the inner sentiment,—in a word, the poetry of childhood. This great achievement would alone entitle him to a place among the grand 'masters of all time' in his art.

The attempt made here,—perhaps rashly,—is to express the sentiment revealed by Reynolds in his pictures of children, as it may have inspired him, consciously or unconsciously, whilst he watched and drew them.

In the smiled: Compare the *sorrise parolette brevi* of Dante: *Paradiso:* c. i.

TRAFALGAR

October 21 : 1805

HEARD ye the thunder of battle
    Low in the South and afar?
Saw ye the flash of the death-cloud
    Crimson on Trafalgar?
Such another day never
    England will look on again,
Where the battle fought was the hottest,
    And the hero of heroes was slain!

For the fleet of France and the force of Spain were gather'd for fight,
A greater than Philip their lord, a new Armada in might:—
And the sails were aloft once more in the deep Gaditanian bay,
Where *Redoubtable* and *Bucentaure* and great *Trinidada* lay;
Eager-reluctant to close; for across the bloodshed to be
Two navies beheld one prize in its glory,—the throne of the sea!

Which were bravest, who should tell? for both were
    gallant and true;
But the greatest seaman was ours, of all that sail'd o'er
    the blue.

From Cadiz the enemy sallied: they knew not Nelson
    was there;
His name a navy to us, but to them a flag of despair.
From Ayamonte to Algeziras he guarded the coast,
Till he bore from Tavira south; and they now must fight,
    or be lost;—
Vainly they steer'd for the Rock and the Midland shelter-
    ing sea,
For he headed the Admirals round, constraining them
    under his lee,
Villeneuve of France, and Gravina of Spain: so they
    shifted their ground,
They could choose,—they were more than we;—and
    they faced at Trafalgar round;
Banking their fleet two deep, a fortress-wall thirty-tower'd;
In the midst, four-storied with guns, the dark *Trinidada*
    lower'd.

So with those.—But meanwhile, as against some dyke that
    men massively rear,
From on high the torrent surges, to drive through the
    dyke as a spear,

Eagle-eyed e'en in his blindness, our chief sets his double
    array,
Making the fleet two spears, to thrust at the foe, any
    way, . . .
'Anyhow!—without orders, each captain his Frenchman
    may grapple perforce:
'Collingwood first' (yet the *Victory* ne'er a whit slacken'd
    her course)
'Signal for action! Farewell! we shall win, but we meet
    not again!'
—Then a low thunder of readiness ran from the decks o'er
    the main,
And on,—as the message from masthead to masthead
    flew out like a flame,
ENGLAND EXPECTS EVERY MAN WILL DO HIS DUTY,—they
    came.

—Silent they come:—While the thirty black forts of the
    foemen's array
Clothe them in billowy snow, tier speaking o'er tier as
    they lay;
Flashes that came and went, as swords when the battle is
    rife;—
But ours stood frowningly smiling, and ready for death as
    for life.

—O in that interval grim, ere the furies of slaughter embrace,
Thrills o'er each man some far echo of England; some glance of some face!
—Faces gazing seaward through tears from the ocean-girt shore;
Features that ne'er can be gazed on again till the death-pang is o'er. . .
Lone in his cabin the Admiral kneeling, and all his great heart
As a child's to the mother, goes forth to the loved one, who bade him depart
. . . O not for death, but glory! her smile would welcome him home!
—Louder and thicker the thunderbolts fall:—and silent they come.

As when beyond Dongola the lion, whom hunters attack,
Stung by their darts from afar, leaps in, dividing them back;
So between Spaniard and Frenchman the *Victory* wedged with a shout,
Gun against gun; a cloud from her decks and lightning went out;
Iron hailing of pitiless death from the sulphury smoke;
Voices hoarse and parch'd, and blood from invisible stroke.

Each man stood to his work, though his mates fell smitten around,
As an oak of the wood, while his fellow, flame-shatter'd, besplinters the ground :—
Gluttons of danger for England, but sparing the foe as he lay;
For the spirit of Nelson was on them, and each was Nelson that day.

'She has struck!'—he shouted—'She burns, the *Redoubtable!* Save whom we can,
'Silence our guns':—for in him the woman was great in the man,
In that heroic heart each drop girl-gentle and pure,
Dying by those he spared :—and now Death's triumph was sure!
From the deck the smoke-wreath clear'd, and the foe set his rifle in rest,
Dastardly aiming, where Nelson stood forth, with the stars on his breast,—
'In honour I gain'd them, in honour I die with them' . . . Then, in his place,
Fell . . . 'Hardy! 'tis over; but let them not know': and he cover'd his face.
Silent, the whole fleet's darling they bore to the twilight below:
And above the war-thunder came shouting, as foe struck his flag after foe.

·To his heart death rose : and for Hardy, the faithful, he
    cried in his pain,—
'How goes the day with us, Hardy?' . . . ' 'Tis ours ':—
    Then he knew, not in vain
Not in vain for his comrades and England he bled : how
    he left her secure,
Queen of her own blue seas, while his name and example
    endure.
O, like a lover he loved her! for her as water he pours
Life-blood and life and love, given all for her sake, and
    for ours!
—'Kiss me, Hardy!—Thank God!—I have done my
    duty!'—And then
Fled that heroic soul, and left not his like among men.

    Hear ye the heart of a nation
        Groan, for her saviour is gone;
    Gallant and true and tender,
        Child and chieftain in one?
    Such another day never
        England will weep for again,
    When the triumph darken'd the triumph,
        And the hero of heroes was slain.

THE DEATH OF SIR JOHN MOORE

January 15 : 1809

HE stood above Elvina; and behind him, where he stood,
On the blue sea fell the sunset, the blue was barr'd with
    blood :
Between the fleet and foe he stood : Before him all the
    crest
Alive with bristling warriors, like hornets round the nest :—
And well that English heart foresaw the toughness of the
    fray,
As, gallant foe 'gainst gallant foe, his army turn'd at bay.

'They have dogg'd us here from Spain, the French! At
    last at bay we stand,
'Forlorn hope of the war, outflank'd, outnumber'd,—not
    outmann'd !
'On, Highlanders !' . . . and o'er the field the dark-green
    tartans flow
As the torrent-spate that bursts in spring, and backward
    roll the foe ;

And right and left they dash them off, as up the brae
    they glide,—
O! what was that sierra to Glencoe or Coolin-side?

The musket gripp'd; the brow firm set; a scowlful smile
    of joy;
And shoulder square by shoulder, as of old at Fontenoy:—
Up! where the battery-flash the heaven with battle-thunder
    stuns,
Where the swarthy cannoneers of France yet prime and
    point their guns,
Then on them with that levell'd steel, one charge . . .
    Too late! . . . the breath
Of war's red throat across the field has borne a waft of
    death.

From his horse it rends the hero, in his heart's own
    fountain bathed;
O'er shatter'd breast hangs shatter'd arm; the soul alone
    unscathed:
Yet he lifts him where he lay; a light of triumph o'er
    his eye;
His comrades safe, the foe thrown back! . . . ''Tis thus
    I long'd to die!

'I cannot live, I know it,'—deep, too deep, 'twas in his breast:
And from the turf they raised him, ready for a soldier's rest.

So they raise him: and the sword-hilt in the wound enhamper'd caught,
The cavern'd wound, life's gaping gate, within his bosom wrought:
And with woman's tender touch the red rough hands that held him, fain
From the heaving breast would draw it forth, and staunch the crimson rain :—
Comrades in fight, ah! part them not, the soldier and his blade!
'But let it leave the field with me; 'tis better so,' he said.

They bore him toward the ramparts, while the fainter, farther, gun,
Of the French within their lines thrust back told him,— the warfare won :—
''Twas thus I ever wish'd to die; and in England I confide;
'She will be just to me! . . . but tell my mother how I died' :—

—And England's heart, as ever, woke, at last, to the true, the brave,
And wreathed a deathless dirge, a crown of music, round his grave.

The advance of Napoleon, who had 300,000 men in Spain, the ruin and general mismanagement of the Spanish armies, compelled Sir John Moore, whose whole force was but 22,000, to retrace his march from Salamanca and Mayorga to the north-western coast. Napier, (*Peninsula War*, B. IV), ably defends the march and the retreat, for which Moore at the time was ungenerously and unjustly blamed. The battle at Corunna was fought to cover the embarkation of the British forces : Soult commanding the French with about 20,000 ; the British not reaching 15,000.

These lines are offered as a modest preface to Wolfe's splendid Elegy : my hope being that his poem may be rendered more interesting when read with a brief record of the battle in which Moore fell.

Elvina: a village in the valley between the lines of hill which each army occupied. The French had a battery on a crest commanding the English right.

On, Highlanders: the famous Forty-second, (called the Black Watch from the colour of their tartans,) who charged the enemy in Elvina at Moore's order. They served at Fontenoy (1745). Moore's death-wound followed immediately. His last words are given by Napier and Southey.

At last: No date is assigned to Wolfe's *Elegy* in the Memoirs of his life. But it had been published (without his name) by Jan : 1822 : (*Medwin : Conversations with Lord Byron*).

TORRES VEDRAS

1810

As who, while erst the Achaians wall'd the shore,
   Stood Atlas-like before,
A granite face against the Trojan sea
   Of foes who seethed and foam'd
From that stern rock refused incessantly;

So He, in his colossal lines, astride
   From sea to river-side,
Alhandra past Aruda to the Towers,
   Our one true man of men
Challenged bold France and all the Imperial powers.

For when that Eagle, towering in his might
   Beyond the bounds of Right,
O'ercanopied Europe with his rushing wings,
   And all the world was prone
Before him as a God, a King of Kings;

When Freedom to one isle, her ancient shrine,
  O'er the free favouring brine
Fled, as a girl by lustful war and shame
  Discloister'd from her home,
Barefoot, with glowing eyes, and cheeks on flame,

And call'd aloud, and bade the realm awake
  To arms for Freedom's sake:
—Yet,—for the land had rusted long in rest,
  The nerves of war unstrung,
Faint thoughts or rash alternate in her breast,

While purblind party-strife with venomous spite
  Made plausible wrong seem right,—
O then for that unselfish hero-chief
  Tender and true, and lost
At Trafalgar,—or him, whose patriot grief

Died with the prayer for England, as he died,
  In vain we might have cried!
But this one pillar rose, and bore the war
  Upon himself alone;
Supreme o'er Fortune and her idle star.

For not by might but mind, by skill, not chance,
    He headed stubborn France
From Tagus back by Douro to Garonne;
    And on the last, worst, field,
The crown of all his hundred victories won,

World-calming Waterloo!—Then, laying by
    War's fearful enginery,
In each state-tempest mann'd the wearying helm;
    E'en through life's winter-years
Serving with all his strength the ungrateful realm.

O firm and foursquare mind! O solid will
    Fix'd, inexpugnable
By crowns or censures! only bent to do
    The day's work in the day;—
Fame with her idiot yelp might come, or go!

O breast that dared with Nature's patience wait
    Till the slow wheels of Fate
Struck the consummate hour; in leash the while
    Reining his eager bands,
The prey in view,—with that foreseeing smile!

And when for blood on Salamanca ridge
    Morn broke, or Orthez' bridge,
He read the ground, and his stern squadrons moved
    And placed with artist-skill,
Like pieces in the perilous game they loved,

Impassive, iron, he and they!—and then
    With eagle-keener ken
Glanced through the field, the crisis-instant knew,
    And through the gap of war
His thundering legions on their victory threw.

Not iron, he, but adamant! Diamond-strong,
    And diamond-clear of wrong:
For truth he struck right out, whate'er befall!
    Above the fear of fear:
Duty for duty's sake his all-in-all.

Among the many wonders of Wellington's Peninsular campaign, from Vimiero (1808) to Toulouse (1814), the magnificent unity of scheme preserved throughout is, perhaps, the most wonderful: the dramatic coherence, development, and final catastrophe of triumph. For this, however, readers must be referred to Napier's *History;* enough here to add that one of the most decisive steps was the formation of the lines in defence of Lisbon, of which the most northerly ran from Alhandra on the Tagus by Aruda and Zibreira to Torres Vedras near the sea-coast at the mouth of the Zizandre.

When Freedom: the unwise and uncertain management of the campaign by the English home Government has been set forth by Napier with so much emphasis as, in some degree, to impair the reader's full conviction. Yet the amazing superiority in energy and wisdom with which Wellington towered over his contemporaries, (the field being, however, cleared by the recent deaths of Nelson and Pitt), is so patent, that this attempt to do justice to his greatness is offered with hesitation and apology.

Orthez' bridge: crosses the river named Gave de Pau;—and covered Soult's forces then lying north of it.

ART AND NATURE:

In Memory of J. M. W. Turner

O! as within thy spell we stand
A spirit thee, not man, I deem;
By Nature her interpreter sent
To realize her ideal dream!
Aethereal stainlessness of sky
By multitudinous vapour fleck'd;
Forest of rhythmic line and curve
With storm-inviolate leafage deck'd.

For she, though duly held divine,
Yet shares not the creative soul;
In atom-elements bound, and bound
By laws e'en she cannot control:—
And ever, in her ceaseless toil
With fruit and flower her world to grace,
A shadow checks the mighty hand,
A death-spot mars the perfect face.

And nearer, ever nearer yet,
The foes of fire and frost move on,
And aye before her eyes is set
The sepulchre of the central sun:
For she is thrall to space and time
'Mid all her radiancy and force;
God's, but not God:—in heartless ease
Completing her aeonian course.

Yet in her children's soul at times
She seems to find herself a soul;
By words or hues when master-hands
From partial beauty frame a whole:—
A forest vale, where Saturn sits,
A vision of the haunted Lake,
A more than Italy, where the waves
With azure smile on Baiae break.

O beatific splendours high
Beyond all mortal sight may view,
Hill heap'd on hill in magic maze,
Plain mix'd with sky in liquid blue;
While, cloud on cloud, and arch o'er arch,
From crimson sea to sapphire height
The sun his rainbow-palace weaves,
Infinities of light in light!

Impassion'd insight into worlds
That Nature dreams but cannot frame!
Thy spell the soul o'er Nature lifts
To prove a wider range and aim!
With eyes that this dim sight outrun
We pass the horizon, limit-free,
While in ourselves we read the pledge
Of man's own immortality.

    The attempt here is to put into words the spirit and effect of Turner's landscape in its most characteristic phase.

    'Nature,' says Sidney in the *Defence of Poesy*, 'never set forth the work in so rich tapestry as divers poets have done; neither with so pleasant rivers, fruitful trees, sweet smelling flowers, and whatsoever else may make the too much loved earth more lovely.'

    Aye before her eyes: See *Garianonum*.

    A forest vale: The allusions here are to the *Hyperion* of Keats, the *Morte d'Arthur* of Tennyson, the glorified Italy to which Turner devoted several masterpieces.

THE VALLEY OF DEATH

1842

WHERE midnight broods o'er the rift
Of the black Suleiman pass,
Ramparts of adamant rock,
And stream frost-smitten to glass:
Where the White Mount looks with ghostly head
O'er Arachosia sunk below,
And his northern beacon Himalah lifts,
An answering blaze of eternal snow:—
In the blank and bleakness of Nature, the frost that strangles the breath,
What torrent,—no torrent,—but heard in the ear of the soul alone,
What triumph of Fate is hurrying on?
—They are coming! Who come?—We are coming!—
through England's valley of death!

The pale riding of Death before;
A phantom rout in the rear;

Glory jostling with Shame,
Blind Courage fetter'd by Fear:
Is it the hiss of the ice-hemm'd stream,
The out-pour of winter-leaves in the glen?
More than the breeze is heard in the breeze;
Army of ghosts that were living men!
Who are here from the city of Ammon's son, from Aornos high?
—Slain in a late revenge for a crime, for a war unjust,
Corpses hidden in Afghan dust,
England's unhappy dead before us in spirit go by.

First-fruit of sacrifice, Burnes,
Like one set fast in a spell,
Scorning the warning of doom,
Gash'd, at his gate as he fell!
Then, a wizard enmesh'd in the web of his net,
Self-limed and slain in the pride of his art,
Macnaghten, perplex'd and pale, and the wound
Of panic-anger, starr'd on the heart;
Happy, not seeing his work of defeat and dismay!—
And then that gray ghost of a chief, worn down and haggard with pain
For the gallant heads 'neath his standard slain,
To the load of command unequal, and gliding apart on his way.

And others I saw, who died
As Englishmen hunger to die,
Paton and Nicholl and Sturt,
The star o'er their heads, go by :—
And then with the cry that rings in the heart
Of silence utter, a myriad rush,
Soul upon soul of women and babes
Stifled and shot in the horrible crush,
As they choked in the jaws of the pass, or, bedded in alien snow,
Sigh'd their faint lives away, and the last sigh froze on the face,—
Far lying there from the graves of the race;
The temples and palms of the sun, where Ganges and Jumna go.

—O fellow-citizen souls
Through whom our warfare we wreak!
O weight of Empire, to dust
Stamping the frail and the weak!
For as the wild things of Nature, shear'd
From the root by the march of the trenchant plough,
To the sun-stain'd immature tribes of man
Engine of extirpation, thou!

Ah Juggernaut car of Advance!—coarse wheels that the
  circle of Fate
Traverse in native blood, and level a solitude-peace :
  While exultant Civilization sees
Her mirage-vision afar,—Utopian perfect State !

   For Nature and Law relentless
   Through the worlds work out their plan,
   Aid or efface impassive :
   But man is the scourge of man !
 —Adamant walls of the black Suleiman,
 Bald eagles that bark in the throat of the pass,
 White mists that serpent-like creep and cling,
 Still frozen torrent, a road of glass ;
Gay feathery firs that wave in the valley of human woe,
Beauty of Nature and terror and waste, ye sought not our
  dead !
 The ruby stream down the torrent-bed,
The victor-victim host,—the shrouding ensanguined snow!

   —Through that ebonine gate of doom
   The thrice five thousand are flown :
   —What sound is now in the silence,
   What footfall echoing lone ?
 Footfall falling slowly, wearily ;
 Human sounds of a human life,

Mazed and dazed atween death and breath,
—The one who out-slipp'd the jezail and the knife!
Is it hap or mishap for him,—sole sad survivor of hosts,
Bent to the mane as he rides, a gasping skeleton white,
—Unseen the red-cross beacon in sight,—
To the City of Refuge he comes, alone, from the valley
of ghosts!

More than sixteen thousand lives, of which the unhappy Indian camp-followers formed the larger number, are given by Kaye in his History of the War in Afghanistan, as lost in the fatal retreat from Caubul between the 6th and the 13th of January, 1842. 'No failure 'so total and overwhelming as this,' he sums up, 'is recorded in 'the page of history.' But for an admirable narrative of the events which led to the disaster, of the ruin and of the revenge, the reader is referred to that work.

Suleiman pass: the two ravines most darkly conspicuous in the retreat, those of Koord-Caubul and Jugdulluck, appear to form part of the Suleiman range; the chief summit of which, the 'White 'Mountain,' commands the valley between Caubul and Jellalabad. The northern side is formed by an offshoot of the Himalah.

Arachosia: ancient name of south-eastern Afghanistan.

City of Ammon's son: Candahar, one of the most easterly among the numerous Alexandrias founded after the campaigns of the great Macedonian.

Aornos: a high rock described by Arrian, and identified by some with Naogee in Bajour.

Burnes: Killed in his own house at Caubul, although warning had been given him, in the riot of Nov. 2, 1841.—Macnaghten, our envoy, who, with Lord Auckland, was most responsible for the unjust conquest which ended in destruction, was pistolled, in a sudden fit of anger, by Akbar Khan at a conference on Dec. 23, 1841.

Ghost of a chief: General Elphinstone, the gallant but most pitiable commander of our forces. He died, (in prison), April 1842. The three officers named fell bravely in the passes.

The one who outlived: Brydon, who reached Jellalabad on Jan. 13, 1842. 'A sentry on the ramparts, looking out towards the ' Caubul road, saw a solitary, white-faced horseman. . . . Slowly ' and painfully, as though horse and rider were both in an extrem- ' ity of mortal weakness, the solitary mounted man came reeling, ' tottering on. . . . A shudder ran through the garrison. . . . ' There was the one man who was to tell the story of the massacre ' of a great army': (*Kaye:* B. VI: ch. iv).

Jezail: heavy Afghan musket.

THE SOLDIERS' BATTLE

November 5 : 1854

In the solid sombre mist
And the drizzling dazzling shower
They may mass them as they list,
The gray-coat Russian power;
They are fifties 'gainst our tens, they, and more!
And from the fortress-town
In silent squadrons down
O'er the craggy mountain-crown
    Unseen, they pour.

On the meagre British line
That northern ocean press'd;
But we never knew how few
Were we who held the crest!
While within the curtain-mist dark shadows loom
    Making the gray more gray,
    Till the volley-flames betray
    With one flash the long array:
    And then, the gloom.

For our narrow line too wide
On the narrow crest we stood,
And in pride we named it *Home*,
As we sign'd it with our blood.
And we held-on all the morning, and the tide
Of foes on that low dyke
Surged up, and fear'd to strike,
Or on the bayonet-spike
Flung them, and died.

It was no covert, that,
'Gainst the shrieking cannon-ball!
But the stout hearts of our men
Were the bastion and the wall :—
And their chiefs hardly needed give command;
For they tore through copse and gray
Mist that before them lay,
And each man fought, that day,
For his own hand!

Yet should we not forget
'Gainst that dun sea of foes
How Egerton bank'd his line,
Till in front a cloud uprose
From the level rifle-mouths; and they dived

With bayonet-thrust beneath;
Clench'd teeth and sharp-drawn breath,
Plunging to certain death,—
    And yet survived!

Nor the gallant chief who led
Those others, how he fell;
When our men the captive guns
Set free they loved so well,
And embraced them as live things, by loss en-
    dear'd :—
Nor, when the crucial stroke
On their last asylum broke,
And e'en those hearts of oak
    Might well have fear'd,—

How Stanley to the fore
The citadel rush'd to guard,
With that old Albuera cry
Fifty-seventh! Die hard!
Yet saw not how his lads clear the crest,
    And, each one confronting five,
    The stubborn squadrons rive,
    And backward, downward, drive,—
        —Death-call'd to rest!

—O proud and sad for thee!
And proud and sad for those
Who on that stern foreign field
Not seeking, found repose,
As for England their life they gladly shed!
Yet in death bethought them where,
Not on these hillsides bare,
But within sweet English air
    Their own home-dead

In a green and mounded peace
Beside God's house are laid :—
Then turn'd to their release
Unhelp'd, unwept, unafraid :—
For they knew that God would count each shatter'd
    limb
Death-torn for England's sake,
And in Christ's own mercy take
On the day when souls shall wake,
    Their souls to Him!

The battle of Inkermann was mainly fought on a ridge of rock which projects from the south-eastern angle of Sebastopol: the English centre of operations being the ill-fortified line named the 'Home Ridge.' The numbers engaged in field-operations, roughly speaking, were 4000 English against 40,000 Russians.

The curtain-mist: The battle began about 6 A.M. under heavy mist and drizzling rain, which lasted for several hours. Through this curtain the Russian forces coming down from the hill were seen only when near enough to darken the mist by their masses.

Egerton: He commanded four companies of the 77th, and charged early in the battle with brilliant success ;—his men, about 250, scattering 1500 Russians.

The gallant chief: General Soimonoff, killed just after Egerton's charge.

With that old Albuera cry: Prominent in the defence of the English main base of operations, the Home Ridge, against a weighty Russian advance, was Captain Stanley, commanding the 57th. This regiment, it was said, at the battle of Albuera had been encouraged by its colonel with the words, 'Fifty-seventh, die-hard':—and Stanley, having less than 400 against 2000, thought the time had come to remind his 'Die-hards' of their traditional gallantry ;—after which he himself at once fell mortally wounded.

AFTER CAWNPORE

June : 1857

FOURTEEN, all told, no more,
Pack'd close within the door
Of that old idol-shrine :
And at them, as they stand,
And from that English band,
The leaden shower went out, and Death proclaim'd them,
Mine !
Fourteen against an army ; they, no more,
Had 'scaped Cawnpore.

With each quick volley-flash
The bullets ping and plash :
Yet, though the tropic noon
With furnace-fury broke
The sulphur-curling smoke,
Scarr'd, sear'd, thirst-silenced, hunger-faint, they stood :
And soon
A dusky wall,—death sheltering life,—uprose
Against their foes.

Behind them now is cast
The horror of the past;
The fort that was no fort,
The deep dark-heaving flood
Of foes that broke in blood
On our devoted camp, victims of fiendish sport;
From that last huddling refuge lured to fly,
—And help so nigh!

Down toward the reedy shore
That fated remnant pour,
Mad Fear and Death beside;
And other spectres yet
Of darker vision flit,—
Old unforgotten wrongs, the harshness and the pride
Of that imperial race which sway'd the land
By sheer command!

O little hands that strain
A mother's hand in vain
With terror vague and vast:—
Parch'd eyes that cannot shed
One tear upon the head,
A young child's head, too bright for such fell death to blast!
Ah! sadder captive train ne'er filed to doom
Through vengeful Rome!

From Ganges' reedy shore
The death-boats they unmoor,
Stack'd high with hopeless hearts;
A slowly-drifting freight
Through the red jaws of Fate,
Death-blazing banks between, and flame-wing'd arrow-
darts:—
Till down the holy stream those cargoes pour
Their flame and gore.

In feral order slow
The slaughter-barges go,
Martyrs of heathen scorn:
While, saved from flood and fire
To glut the tyrant's ire,
The quick and dead in one, from their red shambles borne,
Maiden and child, in that dark grave they throw,
Our well of woe!

O spot on which we gaze
Through Time's all-softening haze,
In peace, on them at peace
And taken home to God!
—O whether 'neath the sod,
Or sea, or desert sand, what care,—when that release
From this dim shadow-land, through pathways dim,
Bears us to Him?

—But those fourteen, the while,
Wrapt in the present, smile
On their grim baffled foe;
Till o'er the wall he heaps
The fuel-pile, and steeps
With all that burns and blasts;—and now, perforce, they go
Hack'd down and thinn'd, beyond that temple-door
But Seven,—no more.

O Elements at strife
With this poor human life,
Stern laws of Nature fair!
By flame constrain'd to fly
The treacherous stream they try,—
And those dark Ganges waves suck down the souls they bear!—
O crowning anguish! Dawn of hope in sight;
Then, final night!

And now, Four heads, no more,
Life's flotsam flung ashore,
They lie :—O not as they
Who o'er a dreadful past
The heart's-ease sigh may cast!

Too worn! too tried!—their lives but given them as a
   prey!
Whilst all seems now a dream, a nought of nought,
   For which they fought!

 —O stout Fourteen, who bled
 O'erwhelm'd, not vanquishéd!
 In those dark days of blood
 How many did, and died,
 And others at their side
Fresh heroes, sprang,—a race that cannot be subdued!
 —Like them who pass'd Death's vale, and lived;—
  the Four
  Saved from Cawnpore!

  The English garrison at Cawnpore, with a large number of sick, women, and children, were besieged in their hastily made and weak earthworks by Nana Sahib from June 6 to June 25, 1857. Compelled to surrender, under promise of safe convoy down the Ganges, on the 27th they were massacred by musketry from the banks; the thatch of the river-boats being also fired. The survivors were murdered and thrown into the well upon Havelock's approach on July 15.
  One boat managed to escape unburnt on June 27. It was chased through the 28th and 29th, by which time the crowd on board was reduced to fourteen men, one of whom, Mowbray-Thomson, has left a narrative equally striking from its vividness and its modesty. Seven escaped from the small temple in which they defended themselves; four only finally survived to tell the story.
  A dusky wall: 'After a little time they stood behind a rampart ' of black and bloody corpses, and fired, with comparative security, ' over this bulwark:' (*Kaye: Sepoy War:* B. V: ch. ii).
  Old unforgotten wrongs: See Appendix.

MOUNT VERNON

October 5 : 1860

BEFORE the hero's grave he stood,
A simple stone of rest, and bare
To all the blessing of the air,
And Peace came down in sunny flood
From the blue haunts of heaven, and smiled
Upon the household reconciled.

—A hundred years have hardly flown
Since in this hermitage of the West
'Mid happy toil and happy rest,
Loving and loved among his own,
His days fulfill'd their fruitful round,
Seeking no more than what they found.

Sweet byways of the life withdrawn!
Yet here his country's voice,—the cry
Of man for natural liberty,—
That great Republic in her dawn,
The immeasurable Future,—broke;
And to his fate the Leader woke.

x

Not eager, yet, the blade to bare
Before the Father-country's eyes,—
—E'en if a parent's rights, unwise,
With that bold Son he grudged to share,
In manhood strong beyond the sea,
And ripe to wed with Liberty!

—Yet O! when once the die was thrown,
With what unselfish patient skill,
Clear-piercing flame of changeless will,
The one high heart that moved alone
Sedate through the chaotic strife,—
He taught mankind the hero-life!

As when the God whom Pheidias moulds,
Clothed in marmoreal calm divine,
Veils all that strength 'neath beauty's line,
All energy in repose enfolds;—
So He, in self-effacement great,
Magnanimous to endure and wait.

O Fabius of a wider world!
Master of Fate through self-control
And utter stainlessness of soul!
And when war's weary sign was furl'd,
Prompt with both hands to welcome in
The white-wing'd Peace he warr'd to win!

Then, to that so long wish'd repose!
The liberal leisure of the farm,
The garden joy, the wild-wood charm;
Life ebbing to its perfect close
Like some white altar-lamp that pales
And self-consumed its light exhales.

Then, as a mother's love and fears
Throng round the child, unseen but felt,
So by his couch his nation knelt,
Loving and worshipping with her tears :—
Tears!—late amends for all that debt
Due to the Liberator yet!

For though the years their golden round
O'er all the lavish region roll,
And realm on realm, from pole to pole,
In one beneath thy stars be bound:
The far-off centuries as they flow,
No whiter name than this shall know!

—O larger England o'er the wave,
Larger, not greater, yet!—With joy
Of generous hearts ye hail'd the boy
Who bow'd before the sacred grave,
With Love's fair freight across the sea
Sped from the Fatherland to thee!

And Freedom on that Empire-throne
Blest in his Mother's rule revered,
On popular love a kingdom rear'd,
And rooted in the years unknown,—
Land rich in old Experience' store
And holy legacies of yore,

And youth eternal, ever-new,—
From the high heaven look'd out:—and saw
This other later realm of Law,
Of that old household first-born true,
And lord of half a world!—and smiled
Upon the nations reconciled.

The date prefixed is that of the visit which the Prince of Wales paid to the tomb of Washington: carrying home thence, as one of the most distinguished of his hosts said, 'an unwritten treaty of 'amity and alliance.'

Mount Vernon on the Potomac, named after the Admiral, was the family seat of Augustine, father to George Washington, and the residence of the latter from 1752. But all his early years also had been spent in that neighbourhood, in those country pursuits which formed his ideal of life: and thither, on resigning his commission as Commander-in-Chief, he retired in 1785; devoting himself to farming and gardening with all the strenuousness and devoted passion of a Roman of Vergil's type. And there (Dec. 1799) was he buried.

Not eager: When the ill-feeling between England and America deepened after 1765, Washington 'was less eager than some others ' in declaring or declaiming against the mother country;' (Mahon: *Hist.* ch. lii).

Ripe to wed with liberty: See Appendix.

Due to the Liberator: Compare the epitaph by Ennius on Scipio :
>Hic est ille situs, cui nemo civi' neque hostis
>>Quivit pro factis reddere opis pretium.

History, it may be said with reasonable confidence, records no hero more unselfish, no one less stained with human error and frailty, than George Washington.

The years unknown: It is to Odin, whatever date be thereby signified, that our royal genealogy runs back.

SANDRINGHAM

1871

IN the drear November gloom
And the long December night,
There were omens of affright,
And prophecies of doom ;
And the golden lamp of life wax'd blue and dim,
   Till Love could hardly mark
   The little sapphire spark
   That only made the dark
     More dark and grim.

There not around alone
'Watch'd sister, brother, wife,
And she who gave him life,
White as if wrought in stone ;
Unheard, invisible, by the bed of death
   Stood eager millions by ;
   And as the hour drew nigh,
   Dreading to see him die,
     Held their breath.

Where'er in world-wide skies
The Lion-Banner burns,
A common impulse turns
All hearts to where he lies :—
For as a babe the heir of that great throne
Is weak and motionless;
And they feel the deep distress
On wife and mother press,
   As 'twere their own.

O! not the thought of race
From Asian Odin drawn
In History's mythic dawn,
Nor what we downward trace,
—Plantagenet, York, Edward, Elizabeth,—
Heroic names approved,—
The blood of the people moved;
But that, 'mongst those he loved,
   He fought with death.

And if the Reason said
' 'Gainst Nature's law and death
' Prayer is but idle breath,'—
Yet Faith was undismay'd,
Arm'd with the deeper insight of the heart :—

Nor can the wisest say
What other laws may sway
The' world's apparent way,
　Known but in part.

Nor knew we on that life
What burdens may be cast;
What issues wide and vast
Dependent on that strife:—
This only:—'Twas the son of those we loved!
That in his Mother's hand
Peace set her golden wand;
'Mid heaving realms, one land
　Law-ruled, unmoved.

—He fought, and we with him!
And other Powers were by,
Courage, and Science high,
Grappling the spectre grim
On the battle-field of quiet Sandringham:
And force of perfect Love,
And the will of One above,
Chased Death's dark squadrons off,
　And overcame.

> —O soul, to life restored
> And love, and wider aim
> Than private care can claim,
> —And from Death's unsheath'd sword!
By suffering and by safety dearer made :—
> O that the life new-found
> With Wisdom's crown be crown'd,
> Till in the common ground
>> Thou too art laid!

A DORSET IDYL:

Holcombe near Lyme

September : 1878

BEFORE me with one happy heave
   Of golden green the hillside curves,
   Where slowly, greenly, rounding swerves
The shadow of each perfect tree,
   By slanting shafts of eve
Flame-fringed and bathed in pale transparency.

And that long ridge that crowns the hill
   Stands fir-dark 'gainst the falling rays ;
   Above, a waft of pearly haze
Lies on the sapphire field of air,
   So radiant and so still
As though a star-cloud took its station there.

Up wold and wild the valley goes,
   'Mid heath and mounded slopes of oak,
   And light ash-thicket, where the smoke
Wreathes high in evening's air serene,
   Floating in white repose
O'er the gray peace of cottage-walls half-seen.

Another landscape at my feet
    Unfolds its nearer grace the while,
    Where gorses gleam with golden smile,
Where Inula lifts a russet head
    The shepherd's spikenard sweet;
And closing Centaury points her rosy red.

One light cicada's simmering cry,
    Survivor of the summer heat,
    Chimes faint; the robin, shrill and sweet,
Pipes from green holly; whilst from far
    The rookery croaks reply,
Hoarse, deep, as veterans readying for war.

—Grief on a happier future dwells;
    The happy present haunts the past;
    And those old minstrels who outlast
Our looser-textured webs of song,
    Nursed in Hellenic dells,
Sicilian, or Italian, hither throng.

Why care if Turk and Tartar fume,
    Barbarian 'gainst barbarian set,
    Or how our politic prophets fret,
When on this tapestry-thyme and heath,
    Fresh work of Nature's loom,
Thus, thus, we can ourselves diffuse, and breathe

Autumnal sparkling freshness?—while
 The page by some bless'd miracle saved
 When Goth and Frank 'gainst Hellas raved
Paints how the wanderer-chief divine,
 Snatch'd from Circaean guile,
Led by Nausicaa past Athéné's shrine,

In that delicious garden sate
 Where summer link'd to summer glows,
 Grapes ever ripe, and rose on rose;
And all the wonders of thy tale
 —O greatest of the great—
Whose splendour ne'er can fade, nor beauty fail!

Or by the city of God above
 In rose-red meadows, where the day
 Eternal burns, the bless'd ones stray;
The harp lets loose its silver showers
 From the dark incense-grove;
And happiness blooms forth with all her flowers.

O Theban strain,—remote and pure,
 Voice of the higher soul, that shames
 Our downward, dry, material aims,
The bestial creed of earth-to-earth,—
 Owning with insight sure
The signs that speak of Man's celestial birth!

Or white Colonos here through green
  Green Dorset winds his holy vale,
  Where the divine deep nightingale
Heaps note on note and love on love,
  In ivy thick unseen,
While goddesses with Dionysos rove.

Another music then we hear,
  A cry from the Sicilian dell,
  'Here 'mid sweet grapes and laurel dwell;
'Slips by from wood-girt Aetna's dome
  'Snow-cold the stream and clear:—
'Hither to me, come, Galataea, come!'

—Voices and dreams long fled and gone!
  And other echoes make reply,
  The low Maenalian melody
''Twas in our garth, a twelve-year child,
  'I saw thee, little one,
'Pick the red fruit that to thy fancy smiled,

'Thee and thy mother: I, your guide:'—
  O sweet magician! Happy heart!
  Content with that unrivall'd art,—
The soul of grace in music shrined,—
  And notes of modest pride,
To sing the life he loved to all mankind!

There, shading pine and torrent-song
  Breathe midday slumber, sudden, sweet;
  Deep meadows woo the wayward feet;
In giant elm the stock-doves moan;
  There, peace secure from wrong,
The life that keeps its promise, there, alone!

—O loftier than the wordy strife
  That floats o'er capitals; the chase
  Of florid pleasure; the blind race
Of gold for gold by gamblers run,
  This fair Vergilian life,
Where heaven and we and nature are at one!

On that deep soil great Rome was sown;
  Our England her foundations laid:—
  Hence, while the nations, change-dismay'd,
To tyrant or to quack repair,
  A healthier heart we own,
And the plant Man grows stronger than elsewhere.

Should changeful commerce shun the shore,
  And newer, mightier races meet
  To push us from our empire-seat,
England will round her call her own,
  And as in days of yore
The sea-girt Isle be Freedom's central throne.

Freedom, fair daughter-wife of Law ;
    One bright face on the future cast,
    One reverent fix'd upon the past,
And that for Hope, for Wisdom this :—
    While counsels wild and raw
Fly her keen eyes, and leave the land to bliss :—

Dear land, where new is one with old :
    Land of green hillside and of plain,
    Gray tower and grange and tree-fringed lane,
Red crag and silver streamlet sweet,
    Wild wood and ruin bold,
And this repose of beauty at my feet :—

Fair Vale, for summer day-dreams high,
    For reverie in solitude
    Fashion'd in Nature's finest mood ;
Or, sweeter yet, for fond excess
    Of glee, and vivid cry,
Whilst happy children find more happiness

Ranging the brambled hollows free
    For purple feast ;—till, light as Hope,
    The little footsteps scale the slope ;
And from the highest height we view
    Our island-girdling sea
Bar the green valley with a wall of blue.

    The poets whose landscape description is here contrasted with English scenery are Homer, Pindar, Sophocles, Theocritus, and Vergil.

THINGS VISIBLE AND INVISIBLE

So far! so very far!
And this life pressing in, for good and ill,
Sea-like at every pore; the tangible
Shrunk round the soul with adamantine bar,
—And that world further than the farthest star!

So long ago! so long!
The world devouring with impassion'd stride
Its history; Years that rather surge, than glide;
Peace with her garish triumphs, and the throng
Of wonders working equal weal and wrong;

Knowledge so free of hand,
Yet vaunting more than she can give or know;
The dazzling Present with his glory-show;
—And that scarce-visible life in Syrian land,
Lost and time-buried by the Dead Sea strand!

  —Strange warfare, which the seen,
The present, wage against the unseen, the past!
As that enchantress, whose sweet guile held fast
Within her palace-walls and forest green
The gray world-wanderer;—though the faithful Queen

  Sate in his island-hall,
And the hearth blazed in winter, and the sun
Shone summer-high above the mountains dun,
As erst before the fatal Spartan call,
And the long siege, and holy Ilion's fall.

  But he remembers nought
Of what has been, and will be:—till the spell
Fade, and his eyes behold the invisible
Long hid:—the faithful wife, the fields he fought,
The signs by Pallas for his safety wrought.

  —We too, amid the glare
Of present life, misdeem the world we view,
Our small horizon, for the boundless blue,
Holding all things must be as now they are,
And our experience valid everywhere.

'Let others tell their tale
'Of wonders by the Hellenic questioning mind
'Accepted:—We ne'er saw the shroud unbind
'Its tenant; nor the cheek change rose for pale,
'Raised up from earth: nor do our powers avail

'To go round Death, and view
'An incorporeal life in realms unseen!
'So let what will be rest with what has been!
'Let the bright Hours their daily dance renew,
'While dreamers chase the Eternal and the True.

'If scanty all we know,
'At least, 'tis science palpable and pure:
'We see!—Thus far, our footsteps are secure:
'No more we ask than sense and senses show,
'And Hope and Faith, vain luxuries, forego.

'The envious Fates on high
'Grudge our horizon, nor will let man stray
'Unpunish'd past the bounds of sentient clay;
'And puff to scorn the adventurers who try
'On self-blown airballs to transcend the sky.

'Man was not made to soar!
'Ascidian-born, not Angel: on this earth
'We clench our sight, nor claim a loftier birth;
'Accept our fate and creep along the shore,
'And with life's music drown the dead-sea roar.'

—To Circe's sleep-soft isle
Straight let us steer, and live by Circe's creed,
If this be all, if this be all, indeed!
—But should our science of things seen, meanwhile,
Have its own bounds and quicksands: Should the smile

Of sceptic doubt assail
The message of the senses; whether things
Be what we see and touch, or imagings
By self on self imposed, without avail
To make us grasp the Infinite, which our frail

Yet eager reason knows
Essential to the scheme of thought, and yet
Transcending thought, because 'tis infinite :—
If beyond Space and Time no science goes,
—Man's limitations, yet to which man owes

The stage whereon he stands
And breathes and thinks and acts :—How then shall man
Cut fragments out from Nature's general plan,
Naming these known, while all beyond he hands
To nescience ?—O fair palace, but on sands,

For all thy bravery, set !—
—To our own selves, O friends, let us be just !
Either not know, or else our knowledge trust :
For all our wisdom, howsoe'er we fret,
Or boast our narrow certainties, is yet

Enframed by hint and guess
And theory :—As when the nights are dark
In Autumn, and men trace a transient arc
That threads its burning way with lightning stress,
And then is swallow'd in blank nothingness,

Deducing from the seen
A credible unseen ; some curve, to roll
Wider for aye, or circle, closed and whole :
—So on our knowledge, partial though, we lean,
And what will be forecast from what has been.

O questioners vaguely bold,
'Tis Reason bids you scorn the facile sneer
That bars the search for truth beyond the sphere!
It is the weak who doubt; the strong who hold
The resolute Faith where new is one with old.

Within a narrow vale
Rock-wall'd and closed, and skies with cloud o'erwrought,
The Powers have planted Man, for life and thought
Knowledge, and love: and, from beyond the pale,
Some bird of God at times above may sail,

Or gleams ascend and go,
As on some castle turret-steps by night
The lamp climbs square by square, and light o'er light:
And then the shameful things of sin and woe,
The poison-plants that in the valley grow,

The sights that in the heart
Tingle, and make us cry, O Lord! how long!
Hast thou forgotten? Why concede such wrong?
Glare with less luridness, and the cloud in part
Thins, and behind we know Thee, that Thou art;—

Justice, and Love, and Law
Eternal.—Madness then, aside to thrust
The heart's unsyllabled voice, the instinctive trust,
The signal-gleams that lighten and withdraw,
Because with mortal sense man never saw

Nor touch'd nor measured God!—
—As that lone sophist of earth's earlier days
Empedocles, who life's common, sunlit, ways
Scorn'd, and the lava layers of Aetna trod,
And dived for light in Typho's red abode:

Nor saw the Immortals rise
Star-eyed around the zenith, when the veil
Of marsh-white mist parts in the midnight gale;
Nor where the dawn above horizon lies,
And Phoebus fluting to the saffron skies.

A SUMMER SUNSET

in South-Western England

    This hour is given to peace :—
The downward-slanting sunbeams graze the vale
Where Even breathes her stealthy gathering gray;
    And o'er white stubble-plots, the sheaves
Like walls of gold stretch out their ripe array.

    Upon the green slope sward
The hedgerow elms lie pencill'd by the sun
In greener greenness: and, athwart the sky,
    Dotted like airy dust, the rooks
Oar themselves homeward with a distant cry.

    And the whole vale beneath,
To Castle Lammas' violet-bosom'd height,
With all its wealth outspread of harvest hopes
    Half green, half russet-gold, runs up
As a fair tapestry shaken o'er the slopes.

      It is an utter calm!
The topmost ash-tree sprays have ceased to wave;
The wood-dove checks her sweet redoubled moan;
      And e'en the gray-wall'd cottages
Sleep 'mid their crofts like things of Nature's own.

      . I hear the shepherd's call;
The white specks gather to the crowding fold,
Their lowly palace of unvex'd repose:
      While o'er the chambers of the sun
Float filmy fleeces of empurpled rose.

      And now the silent moon
Lifts her pale shield above a glassy sea,
And from the highest cloud the sunbeams cease:
      Till, tranced in Nature's holy hour,
The Time-sick heart renews its ancient peace.

      Then in the soul we know
The presence of our dear ones: Love binds up
The sore of life, and pours himself in balm:
      While e'en the memories of the dead
Glide painless through the breast in star-like calm.

A HOME IN THE PALACE

THRICE fortunate he
Who, in the palace born, has early learn'd
The lore of sweet simplicity:
From smiling gold his eyes inviolate turn'd,
Turn'd unreturning:—Who the people's cause,
The sovereign-levelling laws,

Above the throne,
—He made for them, not they for him,—has set;
Life-lavish for his land alone,
Whether she crown with gratitude, or forget:—
He, who in courts beneath the purple weight
Of precedence moves sedate,

By all that glare
Of needful pageantry less stirr'd than still'd,
Bringing a waft of natural air
Through halls with pomp and flattering incense fill'd;
And in the central heart's calm secret, waits
The closure of the gates,

The music mute,
The darkling lamps, the festal tables clear :—
    Then,—glad as one who from pursuit
Breathes safe, and lets himself himself appear,—
Turns to the fireside jest, the laughing eyes,
    The love without disguise,—

    On home alone,
The loyal partnership of man with wife,
    Building a throne beyond the throne;
All happiness in that common household life
By peasant shared with prince,—when toil and health,
    True parents of true wealth,

    To its fair close
Round the long day, and all are in the nest,
    And care relaxes to repose,
And the blithe restless nursery lulls to rest;
Prayer at the mother's knee; and on their beds
    We kiss the shining heads!

    —Thrice fortunate he
Who o'er himself thus won his masterdom,
    Touching that rare felicity
E'en in the palace walls to find the home!
Who shaped his life in calmness, firm and true,
    Each day, and all day through,

To that high goal
Where self, for England's sake, was self-effaced,
In silence reining-in his soul
On the strait difficult line by wisdom traced,
'Twixt gulf and siren, avalanche and ravine,
Guarding the golden mean.

Hence, as the days
Went by, with insight time-enrich'd and true,
O'er Europe's policy-tangled maze
He glanced, and touch'd the central shining clue:
And when the tides of party roar'd and surged,
'Gainst the state-bulwarks urged

By factious aim
Masquing beneath some specious patriot cloke,
Or flaunting a time-honour'd name,—
Athwart the flood he held an even stroke;
Between extremes on her old compass straight
Aiding to steer the state.

With equal mind,
Hence,—sure of those he loved on earth, and then
His loved ones sure again to find,—
For Christ's and England's cause, Goodwill to men,
To the end he strove, and put the fever by,—
Ready to live or die.

—And if in death
We were not so alone, who might not quit,
    Smiling, this tediousness of breath,
These bubble joys that flash and burst and flit,—
This tragicomedy of life, where scarce
    We know if it be farce,

    A puppet-sight
Of nerve-pull'd dolls that o'er the world dance by,
    Or Good in that unequal fight
With Ill . . . who from such theatre would not fly?
—But those dear faces round the bed disarm
    Death of his natural charm!

    —O Prince, to Her
First placed, first honour'd in our love and faith,
    True stay, true constant counseller,
From that first love of boyhood's prime,—to death!
O if thy soul on earth permitted gaze
    In these less-fortunate days

    When, hour by hour,
The million armaments of the world are set
    Skill-weapon'd with new demon-power,
Mouthing around this little isle, . . . and yet
On dream-security our fate we cast,
    Of all that glory-past

With light fool-heart
Oblivious! . . . O in spirit again restored
Insoul us to the nobler part,
The chivalrous loyalty of thy life and word!
Thou, who in Her to whom first love was due,
Didst love her England too,

If earthly care
In that eternal home, where thou dost wait
Renewal of the days that were,
Move thee at all,—upon the realm estate
The wisdom of thy virtue; the full store
Thy life's experience bore!

O known when lost,
Lost, yet not fully known, in all thy grace
Of bloom by cruel early frost,
Best prized and most by Her, to whom thy face
Was love and life and counsel:—If this strain
Renew not all in vain

The bitter cry
Of yearning for the loss we yet deplore,—
Yet for her heart, who stood too nigh
For comfort, till God's hour thy face restore,
Man has no lenitive! . . . He, who wrought the grief
Alone commands relief.

—Thou, as the rose
Lies buried in her fragrance, when on earth
The summer-loosen'd blossom flows,
Art sepulchred and embalm'd in native worth:
While to thy grave, in England's anxious years,
We bring our useless tears.

Above the throne: 'He knows that if Princes exist, it is for the 'good of the people. . . . Well for him that he does so,' was the remark made by an observing foreigner on Prince Albert : (Martin : *Life of H.R.H. the Prince Consort:* ch. xi).

On home alone: 'She who reigns over us,' said the then Mr. Disraeli when seconding the Address on the death of the Duchess of Kent, (March, 1861), 'She who reigns over us has elected, amid 'all the splendour of empire, to establish her life on the principle 'of domestic love :' (*Martin :* ch. cxi).

Firm and true: 'Treu und Fest' is the motto of the Saxe-Coburg family.

Goodwill to men: A revision of the despatch to the United States Cabinet, remonstrating on the 'Trent affair,' whilst the fatal fever was on him, was the last of Prince Albert's many services (Nov. 30, 1861) to England. To the temperate and conciliatory tone which he gave to this message, its success in the promotion of peace between the two countries was largely due : (*Martin:* ch. cxvi).

ENGLAND ONCE MORE

OLD if this England be
The Ship at heart is sound,
And the fairest she and gallantest
That ever sail'd earth round!
And children's children in the years
Far off will live to see
Her silver wings fly round the world
Free heralds of the free!
 While now on Him who long has bless'd
 To bless her as of yore
  Once more we cry for England,
   England once more!

They are firm and fine, the masts;
And the keel is straight and true;
Her ancient cross of glory
Rides burning through the blue:—
And that red sign o'er all the seas
The nations fear and know,

And the strong and stubborn hero-souls
That underneath it go :—
> While now on Him who long has bless'd
> To bless her as of yore
> Once more we cry for England,
> > England once more!

Prophets of dread and shame,
There is no place for you,
Weak-kneed and craven-breasted,
Amongst this English crew!
Bluff hearts that cannot learn to yield,
But as the waves run high,
And they can almost touch the night,
Behind it see the sky.
> While now on Him who long has bless'd
> To bless her as of yore
> Once more we cry for England,
> > England once more!

As Past in Present hid,
As old transfused to new,
Through change she lives unchanging,
To self and glory true;

From Alfred's and from Edward's day
Who still has kept the seas,
To him who on his death-morn spoke
Her watchword on the breeze!
    While now on Him who long has bless'd
    To bless her as of yore
    Once more we cry for England,
        England once more!

What blasts from East and North,
What storms that swept the land
Have borne her from her bearings
Since Caesar seized the strand!
Yet that strong loyal heart through all
Has steer'd her sage and free,
—Hope's armour'd Ark in glooming years,
And whole world's sanctuary!
    While now on Him who long has bless'd
    To bless her as of yore
    Once more we cry for England,
        England once more!

Old keel, old heart of oak,
Though round thee roar and chafe

All storms of life, thy helmsman
Shall make the haven safe!
Then with Honour at the head, and Faith,
And Peace along the wake,
Law blazon'd fair on Freedom's flag,
Thy stately voyage take:—
    While now on Him who long has bless'd
    To bless thee as of yore
    Once more we cry for England,
        England once more!

APPENDIX

THE DIRGE OF LLYWELYN

Where a king: The war in which Llywelyn fell was the inevitable result of the growing power of England under Edward I; and, considering the vast preponderance of weight against the Welsh Prince, it could not have ended but in the conquest of Wales. Yet its issue was determined as if by chance. Llywelyn had left North Wales in the winter of 1282 under a treacherous invitation (it was said) to Builth in Brecon : where he found himself confronted by Sir E. Mortimer who, with the Earl of Gloucester, was in command of a detached force from Edward's main army. Wishing to return home, Llywelyn ascended the Vale of the Irvon (an affluent of the Wye), crossing it a little above Llanynis Church over the Pont y Coed. Here a knight named Walwyn came suddenly on him as he waited with a few followers, and the Prince fell by a chance thrust from one de Frankton in the dell hence named Cwm Llywelyn. On finding whom he had slain, Frankton carried the head to Edward at Rhuddlan, who, with a barbarity unworthy of himself, set it over the Tower of London, wreathed in mockery of a prediction (ascribed to Merlin) upon the coronation of a Welsh Prince in London.

PRINCE CHARLES AT THE LOUVRE

From gay Montreuil: This incident occurred on the romantic and unwise expedition made by Prince Charles and Buckingham to Spain, in prosecution of the prince's intended marriage with the Infanta Maria, second daughter to Philip III. Landing at Boulogne on Feb. 19, 1623, they rode by Montreuil to Paris, and managed an *incognito* admission to a masque rehearsed at court. The wish to see Anne, wife to Louis XIII, and elder sister to the Infanta

Maria, was probably one inducement. 'Of his future wife Charles
' seems to have taken little notice. *There danced*, he wrote, . . .
' *the queen and madame, with as many as made up nineteen fair*
' *dancing ladies ; amongst which the queen is the handsomest, which*
' *hath wrought in me a greater desire to see her sister :*' (Gardiner's
Prince Charles and the Spanish Marriage : ch. xi).

Madame here is the Princess Henrietta. She does not appear to have noticed Charles ; but said afterwards with a sigh that the Prince of Wales need not have gone so far as Madrid to look for a wife. And the Queen (Anne) is said to have regretted that Henrietta was only seen by the Prince at a distance, and in a dim light unfavourable to her beauty.

The 'Spanish Match,' after doing much injury to Charles and his father, was broken off. But the marriage with Henrietta (1625) is said to have been first suggested by her elder sister Elizabeth, Queen of Philip IV.

AFTER CHALGROVE FIGHT

Doth he now . . . : Hampden and Pym, says Hallam (*Const. Hist.* ch. ix), were not only most forward in all the proceedings which brought 'on the war, but among the most implacable oppo-
' nents of all overtures towards reconciliation.' And that the final rupture between the parties in 1642 was determined by the revolutionary character of the demands made by Parliament is the verdict of the calm and careful Ranke. He has stated the successive steps with clearness and impartiality (IX : i) : his general view thus conforming to that of Hallam, that in this great struggle the case for the King was the least unsatisfactory : 'much peril of despotism
' on the one hand, more of anarchy on the other.' How anarchy led by a natural and well-trodden path to 'a despotism compared
' to which all the illegal practices of former kings, all that had cost
' Charles his life and crown; appeared as dust in the balance,' (*Hallam*)—happily for Hampden, unless we are to reject the estimate which has been commonly formed of his character,—was not displayed until the Protectorate reached its most developed stage, ten or twelve years after 1643.

Heroes both : 'Wentworth,' says R. Gardiner, *sub ann.* 1629,
' seemed to himself to be contending for the old and undoubted
' liberties of Englishmen, for their right to freedom from vexatious
' injustice. He was standing in the ancient paths. His knowledge

'of history told him how a Henry II and an Edward I, a Henry
' VIII and an Elizabeth, had actually guided a willing people. It
' told him nothing of a dominant House of Commons reducing its
' Sovereign to insignificance.' Nor, however satisfied the history
of two centuries may leave us, of the essential defects in this theory,
was it,—to be just to Strafford,—wanting in great and recent precedent: for Mr. Gardiner truly remarks that his 'conception of the
' constitution was in the main the same as Bacon's:'—we might
add, as Elizabeth's.

Each his side: 'No one,' says Ranke (whom I must often quote,
because to this distinguished foreigner we owe the only narrative of
this period known to me in which history is treated *historically*,
that is, without judging of the events by the light either of their
remote results, or of modern political party), 'will make any very
' heavy political charge against Strafford on the score of his govern-
' ment of Ireland, or of the partisan attitude which he had taken
' up in the intestine struggle in England in general; for the ideas
' for which he contended were as much to be found in the past
' history of England as were those which he attacked.' And again:
' His defence, which was based on the distinction between the cir-
' cumstances of England and Ireland, had in general more truth
' than the prosecution, which treated Irish events in the same way
' as if they had happened in England': (vii. 6: viii. 3).

A CHURCHYARD IN OXFORDSHIRE

King or nation: The inveterate habit of regarding our past
history, and especially that of the seventeenth century, from the
point of view and with the passions of our own political interests,
so eloquently exposed and resolutely followed by Macaulay, has
poisoned the histories of that period, and prejudiced the readers, to
such a degree, that the attempt here made to maintain an even
balance can only hope to recommend itself to impartial students.
Yet if the great struggle be patiently studied, the moral praise and
censure so freely given, according to a reader's personal bias, will
be found very rarely justified. There was far, very far, less of
tyranny or of liberty involved in the contest up to 1642 than partisans aver. To the actual actors (not as retrospectively criticized by
us) it is a fair battle on both sides, not a contest between light and
darkness. The question simply was, 'whether the King or Parlia-
' ment was to be supreme in the State' (*Gardiner: sub ann.* 1635).

However advantageous to England we may judge the establishment of parliamentary and popular supremacy, our present estimate of these results gives us no clue towards unravelling the history of that struggle, in which facts compel us to recognize that each side was fairly and fully entitled to its own aim and attitude: Charles to claim and exercise, if he could, the royal prerogatives of the last century and a half; parliament to regain its earlier rights and those which the progress of England made it now appear reasonable to the Houses to require in addition. The impartial Ranke notes that the contest, even if embittered by the signal unwisdom of the king, was, in fact, inevitable. The first step of the first Parliament of Charles I (June 1625), disclosed the impracticability of the situation : the leading demand upon the king being that he should put in force the persecuting laws against the Catholics. Not to speak of the higher considerations of religious freedom and humanity, this course was rendered impossible to Charles by his recent marriage and by his conviction, (which no one now is likely to dispute), 'that the House of Commons was ' not a court for deciding ecclesiastical questions. . . . The opposi-
' tion between parliament and the crown . . . in its main principles
' appears immediately after the accession of Charles I, as a histori-
' cal necessity : (*Ranke:* v. 6).

With glory he gilt : Yet to readers, (if such readers there be) who can look with an undazzled eye on military success, Cromwell's foreign policy will be far from supporting the credit with which rhetorical partisanship has invested it.

Holland was beyond question the natural ally on political and religious grounds of puritan England. But a mischievous war against her in 1652-3 was caused by the arrogant restrictions of the Navigation Act of 1651. The successful English demand in 1653 that the Orange family, as connected closely with that of Stuart, should be excluded from the Stadtholdership, was in a high degree to the prejudice of the Commonwealth.

In 1654 Cromwell was negotiating with France and Spain. From the latter he arrogantly asked wholly unreasonable terms, whilst Mazarin, on the part of France, offered Dunkirk as a bribe. News opportunely arriving that certain Spanish possessions in America were feebly armed, Cromwell at once declared war : and now, supplementing dubious policy by false theology, announced ' the Spaniards to be the natural and ordained enemies of England, ' whom to fight was a duty both to country and to religion :' (*Ranke:* xii. 6).

APPENDIX

The piratical war which followed, in many ways similar to that which the 'wise Walpole' tried to avert in 1739, was hardly less impolitic than immoral. It alienated Holland, it sanctioned French aggression on Flanders (xii. 7), it ended by giving Mazarin and Lewis XIV that supremacy in Western Europe for which England had to pay in the wars of William III and Anne; whilst, as soon as it was over, France naturally allied herself with Spain, on a basis which might have caused the union of the two crowns (xii. 8) and which allowed Spain at once to support Charles II. As the result of the protector's 'spirited policy' England thus appeared as the catspaw of France, and the enemy of European liberty.

It is satisfactory, however, to find that, in Ranke's judgment, the common modern opinion that Cromwell's despotism was favourably regarded in England because of his foreign enterprize, is exaggerated. Even against the conquest of Jamaica,—his single signal gain,—unanswerable arguments were popularly urged at the time: (xii. 4, 8).—No portion of our history has been hitherto more mishandled than the Protectorate.

THE MOURNING MUSES

The departed treasures: 'It was necessary that the old estates of
' the crown should serve for carrying on the war against it. The
' royal gardens and castles were sold. The incomparable collection
' of works of art, which Charles I had got together with judgment
' and success, was alienated and broken up. Especially in Spain
' advantage was taken of so favourable a moment for acquiring on
' easy terms such invaluable treasures. . . In England at this time
' [1651] nothing was cultivated but a taste for power and war.
' Since many Cathedrals stood empty, an inquiry was made how
' many could be dispensed with. It was resolved to pull them
' down, and to sell the materials:' (Ranke: *History of England:*
B. xi : ch. iv).

The collection of the Duke of Mantua, according to Dr. Waagen, formed the main strength of Charles'; and as it ranked only next to the Medicean collection, the loss inflicted on England by the barbarous folly of the bigots who sold it may be in some degree imagined. Among the 1387 pictures catalogued, (although many have not been identified), we find thirteen given to Raphael, nine by Correggio, forty-five by Titian, six by Rubens. The sale was in 1653; the large Holy Family by Raphael (from Mantua), purchased for £2,000, was named the *Pearl* by Philip IV, when it reached

Madrid; the beautiful *Peace*, painted by Rubens in England (sold for £100), after wandering to Genoa, was finally bought by Lord Stafford, and presented to the National Gallery, which has also regained Correggio's *Education of Cupid*. In the Louvre are Correggio's *Antiope*; Giorgione's lovely Holy Family with Saints; Titian's *Entombment* and *Emmaus*. The *Saint George*, painted by Raphael for Henry VIII by order of the Duke of Urbino, is in Russia. Readers who desire more details on this curious subject are referred to Waagen's 'Art-treasures in Great Britain.'

Cromwell's destruction of Basing House, which appears to have been a museum of costly works of art, and Fairfax's of the Library of Raglan Castle (1645), are conspicuous instances of the barbarism which this poem deplores. But how much of irrecoverable value to literature and art perished, at this time, by bigotry and violence, cannot, of course, be now traced. It is one of the worst evils of war that it annuls the testimonies to its own destructiveness.

THE RETURN OF LAW

Drill and accustom himself to humility: Upon that most interesting and intricate problem, the character of Cromwell, I have here endeavoured to throw light from many sources, without hoping to solve it. Meanwhile, I add a few remarks from a singularly acute and weighty analyst of character. 'Cromwell had a great mastery
' over the feelings of humility. He not only adopted its language,
' but threw himself into its sensations. He carried about with him
' a large protective machinery of sentiment, under which his strength
' acted with greater freedom and security... There appears to be in
' some minds what we may term the talent of humility, as distin-
' guished from the virtue. This does much more than simply use ex-
' pressions;... it assumes the real feeling,... it creates its sensa-
' tions, and throws itself into its spirit.... Cromwell exhibits
' this talent in a remarkable and highly-developed form. He
' luxuriates in it.... At the time that he was literally riding
' roughshod, with his Ironsides, over the country, he and his
' followers were *the poor, despised, jeered saints; if not sheep, yet*
' *lambs*. They were *poor despised things, poor instruments*. He *did*
' *not grasp at power:* he *would rather have kept a flock of sheep than*
' *held the protectorate:*' (Mozley: *Essay on Carlyle's Cromwell*).

The sky by a veil: 'A spiritual world over and above this in-
' visible one, is a most important addition to our idea of the
' universe; but it does not of itself touch our moral nature....

APPENDIX. 345

' Its moral effect depends entirely upon what we make that world
' to be.'—Cromwell's religion, which may be profitably studied in
his letters and speeches, (much better known of, than read) reveals
itself there as the simple reflex of his personal views : it had great
power to animate, little or none to regulate or control his impulses.
He had, indeed, a most real and pervading 'natural turn for the
' invisible; he thought of the invisible till he died; but the cloudy
' arch only canopied a field of human aim and will :' (*Mozley*).

The horrible sacrament: The summary of Cromwell's conduct
at Drogheda by a writer of so mnch research, impartiality, and
philosophic liberality as Lecky deserves to be well considered.

'The sieges of Drogheda and Wexford, and the massacres that
' accompanied them, deserve to rank in horror with the most
' atrocious exploits of Tilly and Wallenstein, and they made the
' name of Cromwell eternally hated in Ireland. It even now acts
' as a spell upon the Irish mind, and has a powerful and living
' influence in sustaining the hatred both of England and Protestant-
' ism. The massacre of Drogheda acquired a deeper horror and a
' special significance from the saintly professions and the religious
' phraseology of its perpetrators, and the town where it took place
' is, to the present day, distinguished in Ireland for the vehemence
' of its Catholicism :' (*Hist. of Eighteenth Cent.* ch. vi).

If Mr. Lecky's evidence be dismissed, with the common logic
of party, as that of an Irishman, that of the philosophical Ranke
may be weighed : 'Scenes like this are hardly to be explained
' even by fanaticism. But with the heat of Cromwell's zeal
' there are throughout mingled a cold-blooded calculation and
' deliberate violence. . . . No doubt the cruelty with which these
' conquests,' Drogheda and Wexford, 'were accompanied impelled
' commanders or garrisons in one or two fortified places to a speedier
' submission; but these bloody hostilities had yet another unlooked-
' for result. The religious and national hatred between English
' and natives . . . now revived in its full strength :' (Ch. xi. 2).

Mortal failure: The ever-increasing unsuccess of Cromwell's
career is forcibly set forth by Ranke (xii. 8). He had 'crushed
' every enemy,—the Scottish and the Presbyterian system, the
' peers and the king, the Long Parliament and the Cavalier in-
' surgents, but to create . . . an organization consistent with the
' authority which had fallen to his own lot, was beyond his power.
' Even among his old' Anabaptist and Independent 'friends, his
' comrades in the field, his colleagues in the establishment of the
' Commonwealth, he encountered the most obstinate resistance.

'... At no time were the prisons fuller; the number of political prisoners was estimated at 12,000 ... The failure of his plans soured and distracted him.' To the disquiet caused by constant attempts against Cromwell's life, Ranke adds the death of his favourite daughter, Lady Claypole, whose last words of agony 'were of the right of the king, the blood that had been shed, the revenge to come.'

Brought back to Whitehall, he died on the 3rd of September, the 'anniversary of his victories of Dunbar and Worcester, which had gained him this lodging. The people declared that he was snatched away amid the tumult of a fearful storm, a proof that he was in league with Satanic powers. Others saw in it the sympathy of nature with the death of the first man in the world.' But, however able, it had been 'beyond his power, to consolidate a tolerably durable political constitution. His was at best but a *de facto* authority, depending for its existence on the force of arms and his own personal character. Such as it was, it was felt to be an oppressive burden at home no less' by the lovers of 'the old legitimate forms' than by his own party: 'abroad by those who feared him, and by those who were his allies:' (*Ranke:* xii. 8).

THE POET'S EUTHANASIA

Phoebus' wrath: Milton's magnificent version of the cause of his blindness, in the second sonnet to Cyriack Skinner, naturally ignores the fact which his recent biographers confess, that his political pamphlets, so far as can be now judged, were of imperceptible weight in the actual politics of the day. Yet it is singular to find how absolutely he was ignored by the leading army-chiefs and politicians of the Commonwealth; some of whom have their best monument in those splendid lines, which are often so much at variance with the characters and abilities assigned to those whom they commemorate by impartial history.

Since his: The supremacy in rank which this poem ventures to limit to seven poets only (though with a strong feeling of diffidence in view of certain other Hellenic and Roman claims), is assigned to Sappho and Archilochus, less on account of the scanty fragments, though they be 'more golden than gold,' which have reached us, than in confidence that the place collateral with Homer, given them by their countrymen (who criticized as admirably as they created), was, in fact, justified by their poetry.

A DIRGE OF REPENTANCE

Then horrors on horrors: For two centuries, not to go back to Danish, Norman, and Plantagenet days, English rule in Ireland is a picture from which confiscation, bloodshed, and civil or religious persecution, are rarely wanting. In the Elizabethan campaigns ' the suppression of the native race was carried on with a ferocity ' which surpassed that of Alva in the Netherlands. . . . Not only ' the men, but even the women and children were deliberately and ' systematically butchered.'—On a line of 120 miles in Munster not a living soul was to be seen : the wolves themselves lay famished : and it is stated on high English authority, that in six months (1582) more than 30,000 people had been starved to death in that province. ' Even after all resistance had ceased, soldiers forced men and ' women into old barns, which were set on fire : soldiers were seen ' to take up infants on the points of their spears : on one occasion ' some English officers saw three small children feeding off the flesh ' of their starved mother :' (Condensed from *Lecky* : ch. vi).

Nor were these brutalities confined to the Tudor and Stuart rulers : Ludlow, whose Puritanism is beyond reproach, 'relates,' 1652, ' how by pouring in smoke he gained possession of a cave, ' in which a number of Irish believed themselves safe : all in it ' were stifled except a few, who then came out with crucifixes in ' their hands :' (*Ranke* : xi. 4).

Babes snatch'd off: ' The Post-Revolution legislation on the ' subject of Catholic education may be briefly described, for it ' amounted simply to universal, unqualified, and unlimited pro- ' scription.' Schools were indeed established in 1733 : ' but these ' schools were avowedly intended, by bringing up the young as ' Protestants, to extirpate the religion of their parents. The ' alternative offered by law to the Catholics was that of absolute ' and compulsory ignorance, or of an education directly subversive ' of their faith :' (*Lecky: Hist.* ch. ii).

The miseries and the persecutions endured by the poor children in these schools are indescribable : and the determined proselytism in the interest of which they were founded and worked was felt, (and to their honour), by the Roman Catholics ' more keenly than many ' of the measures against their faith which have obtained the largest ' place in Irish history.' Lecky adds an anecdote which might rouse the sympathetic smile of Mephistopheles : ' Sometimes the children ' were quite old enough to have confirmed religious convictions,

' and an eye-witness stated how, not unfrequently, on Fridays or
' other fast days, they *would not use the broth, prepared with meat
' as it was, and it used to be poured down their throats against their
' will:*' (*Hist.* ch. vii).

Caesar-Attila : The discreditable attempt made recently by more than one writer, in defiance of history and common human feeling, to whitewash or glorify the misdeeds committed by the English Government on the Irish between 1642 and 1658 renders it necessary to place the truth before readers, who may have been thus deceived. Upon Drogheda a note will be found elsewhere. That was a rare, though not a solitary, instance of military excess. But Cromwell's savage rule, as, indeed, is notorious, 'planted in the
' Irish mind a hatred of Protestantism and a hatred of England,
' which is even now far from extinguished' : And 'as the civil war
' went on, it became an object of the first political importance to
' the puritan party, and especially to the English Parliament, to
' prevent the reconciliation of the King with the Catholics, and to
' excite the English people to a war of extermination against the
' Irish. Besides this, the Lords Justices, and crowds of hungry
' adventurers, saw with keen delight the opportunity of obtaining
' that general confiscation of Irish lands at which they had been
' so long and so flagitiously aiming :' (*Lecky:* ch. vi). And it should be noted, that although Strafford's attempt to confiscate lands in Connaught 'was made one of the grounds of his impeach-
' ment,' yet the Commons in their declaration concerning the Irish Rebellion 'made it a ground of complaint against the King that he
' had allowed the Connaught proprietors to compound with him
' for their estates :' (*Prendergast*).

For details of the mode in which the Irish rising of 1641 was suppressed by the parliamentary forces under orders from the Lords Justices, readers anxious to know facts are referred to Prendergast's *Cromwellian Settlement of Ireland*, (1870), ch. ii. But as such readers are infrequent, a few extracts may be given. Thus, in Dec. 1641, the English troops, finding a crowd of unarmed clowns,
' rushing out with horse and foot completely armed, slew man,
' woman, and child. The Lords Justices were known not to favour
' any officer that did not, upon his return from these *birdings*,
' as they called them, give a good account of their sport.' In March following, Sir Simon Harcourt took the castle of Carrickmines. 'The besiegers put man, woman, and child, to death, over
' 260 in number—and a priest, being afterwards found hidden in a
' hogshead, they cut him as small as flesh for the pot. This was

APPENDIX 349

' their own boast ! Sir C. Coote went into the suburbs of Dublin
' and the County of Wicklow on like expeditions. His soldiers
' had orders to spare no infants above a span long ';—and an admir-
ing friend thus honoured his memory—

> He by good advice
> Did kill the nitts, that they might not grow lice.

Prendergast's account of this Rebellion substantially agrees with Lecky's, and (like his) proves that the *onus* of blame must fall on the victors, who followed up their crimes by a systematic perversion of the facts which, it may be hoped, is without parallel in history.

The Cromwellian war ended in 1652. More than two-fifths of the population, according to Sir W. Petty, had been destroyed by the sword, by plague, or by famine artificially produced. Fierce wolves might be seen prowling in woods within a few miles of Dublin. Nor was this the worst ; for 'slave-dealers were let loose
' upon the land, and many hundreds of boys and of marriageable
' girls, guilty of no offence whatever, were shipped to Barbadoes,
' and sold as slaves to the planters. The victims appear to have
' been for the most part the children or the young widows of those
' who were killed or starved. How many of the unhappy captives
' became the prey of the sharks, how many became the victims of
' the planters' lusts, it is impossible to say :' (*Lecky : Hist.* ch. vi).

This arrangement was hypocritically described at the time as 'a
' benefit to the people removed, who might thus be made English
' and Christians :' (*Prendergast*) : nor has it wanted its tribute of admiration from a modern writer, who specifies it in his general eulogy of what, in regard to unhappy Ireland, he characteristically terms 'the heroisms of Oliver Protector and his Puritans.'

Broke the pledges of freedom : The gross violation of the religious article of the Treaty of Limerick is notorious. Lord Macaulay, who devotes several pages, in the somewhat tedious manner of his later work, to the Land Redemption Bill of 1700, preserves here that unhappy silence which even this great writer cannot always resist, when *suppressio veri* is required by party considerations. Burke and Hallam express themselves upon this persecution with just indignation. Burke asks ' whether, on that account, there is
' a single right of nature or benefit of society which has not been
' either totally taken away or considerably impaired ':—Hallam's summary is, 'To have exterminated the Catholics by the sword,
' or expelled them, like the Moriscoes of Spain, would have been
' little more repugnant to justice and humanity, but incomparably

' more politic.'—Yet the latter writer, unfair to his own natural impartiality, omits to bring home to his readers the fact that for the earliest of these intolerant breaches of national faith William III permitted himself to be responsible. Lecky, with more courage, remarks (*Hist.* ch. ii.) :

'William was a cold and somewhat selfish man, and the admir-
' able courage and tenacity which he invariably displayed when his
' own designs and ambitions were in question were seldom or never
' manifested in any disinterested cause ; but he was at least eminently
' tolerant and enlightened. . . . It must be observed, however,
' that William, who repeatedly refused his assent to English acts
' which he regarded as inimical to his authority, never offered any
' serious or determined opposition (never chose to risk the unpopu-
' larity of refusing his assent,' he elsewhere says) 'to the anti-
' Catholic laws which began in his reign.'

The obstinacy and blindness of the prejudices of race, especially when combined with religious prejudice, are, I apprehend, nowhere more eminently and more lamentably exhibited than in the field of Irish history. It seems almost impossible that it should be written, or judged, with decent impartiality by an Englishman. Even the recognized ability, brilliancy, and research of Mr. Lecky have failed, thus far, to secure a moderately fair hearing for his invaluable chapters on Ireland.

AT HURSLEY IN MARDEN

Unheirlike heir : Richard Cromwell has received double measure of that censure which the world's judgment too readily gives to unsuccess, finding favour neither from Royalists nor Cromwellians. Macaulay, with more justice, remarks, 'That he was a good man
' he evinced by proofs more satisfactory than deep groans or long
' sermons, by humility and suavity when he was at the height of
' human greatness, and by cheerful resignation under cruel wrongs
' and misfortunes.' . . . 'He did nothing amiss during his short
' administration.'

His fall may be traced to several causes : the puritan party proper, who supported him, the 'sober men' mentioned by Baxter 'that called his father no better than a traitorous hypocrite,' had not power to resist the fanatic cabal of army chiefs : the necessity he was under of protecting some justly-odious confederates of Oliver : his own want of ability or energy to govern,—a fact fully recognized during Oliver's supremacy; and to his own honourable decision not to 'have a drop of blood shed on his poor account.' Yet Richard, had he chosen, might have made a struggle to retain the throne sufficient, at least, to have thus deluged the kingdom : for against the English army gathered about London, on his side were his brother Henry with the troops in Ireland ; Monk (before May, 1659) in Scotland ; Montague and the fleet ; Lockhart and the troops in Flanders ; with the great body of English Presbyterians behind, and energetic offers of men and money from the French government.

Richard obtained Hursley through his marriage (1649). That he was much in debt when he abdicated is certain ; it is more difficult to understand why this was so, when we look at the enormous landed estates which he inherited from his father. His life was passed in great quiet after 1660: Charles II, according to Clarendon, with a wise and humorous lenity, not thinking it 'necessary to ' inquire after a man so long forgotten.' His letters reveal a man of affectionate and honest disposition ; he uses the Puritan phraseology of the day without leaving a sense of nausea in the reader's mind. At Hursley he was buried at a good old age in 1712.

CHARLES EDWARD AT ROME

From central Derby: The decline of public spirit in England, and the apathy which was shown in 1745, are astonishing. 'England,' wrote Henry Fox, 'is for the first comer:' and then, 'Had 5000 ' French ' landed in any part of this island a week ago, I verily believe ' the entire conquest of it would not have cost them a battle.' Lord Hardwicke's testimony in 1749 is similar : ' What a faint resistance ' did the people make in any part of the Kingdom !—so faint that ' had we not been so lucky as to procure a number of regular troops ' from abroad time enough to oppose their approach, they might ' have got possession of our capital without any opposition except ' from the few soldiers we had in London :' (*Lecky: Hist.* ch. iii). —These quotations strengthen Lord Mahon's view as to the great probability of the Prince's success, had not his march on London been defeated by the Council of War at Derby.

A nation's craven rage: The apathy and panic of the nation found their natural issue in the sanguinary punishment of the followers of Prince Charles. 'The city and the generality,' wrote H. Walpole in Aug. 1746, 'are very angry that so many rebels have 'been pardoned.' The vindictive cruelty then shown makes, in truth, (if we compare the magnitude and duration of the rebellions for which punishment was to be exacted), an unsatisfactory contrast with the leniency of 1660. But History supplies only too numerous proofs that a century's march in civilization may be always undone at once by the demons of Panic or of Party in the hour of their respective triumphs.

AFTER CAWNPORE

Old unforgotten wrongs: To the 'History of the Sepoy War in 'India, 1857–1858' by J. W. Kaye,—a narrative equally able and vivid,—the reader must be referred for a singularly lucid and moderate statement of the long series of causes which led to this rebellion. The name 'mutiny,' commonly applied, masks the true nature of the rising, the great determining causes of which lay deep, unhappily, in the history of our Indian Empire. The evidence brought by Kaye seems to render it indisputable that the two major influences most operative in 1857 were the unsympathy between the English, (as a rule, though admitting some noble exceptions), and the natives, —and the enormous annexations of territory made by Lord Dalhousie as Governor General (1848–1856). By the theory of *Lapse*, which set aside native law as recognized by the former Governments, were confiscated Sattarah (1848); Bithoor,—where the native claim was vested in Nana Sahib,—(1852); Jhansi (1853); Nagpore (1854); the Carnatic (1854); Tanjore (1855). Add to this the Land-resumptions, (analogous to the revival of crown-forest-claims by Charles I) in Bombay (1852–1857); with the great absorptions of the Punjaub (1849) and Oude (1856),—both, it should be noticed, against the judgment of the greater of the two great brothers who bore the name Lawrence. But I can only indicate here what any reader, anxious, as every Englishman should be, to understand, (even in the faint degree open to those who have not lived in India), our vast responsibilities, opportunities, and perils in the East, may (I hope) be induced to study and study again, for himself.

MOUNT VERNON

Ripe to wed with Liberty: Looking at the American War of Independence without party-passion and distortion, as should now, at least, be possible to us, the main cause must be recognized to lie simply in the growth and geographical position of the Colonies, which had brought them to the age of natural liberty :—a fact the non-recognition of which by the Fatherland was equally in accordance with nature. For the causes which gradually determined American resistance we must look, (as regards us), not to the blundering English legislation after 1760, but to the whole course of our commercial policy since the Revolution : as regards the Colonies, to the extinction of the power of France in America by the Treaty of Paris in 1763 : (*Lecky* : ch. v ; *Mahon* : ch. xliii).

The Stamp Act of 1765 brought home, indeed, to a rapidly-developing people the supremacy claimed across the Atlantic ; but the obnoxious taxation which it imposed cannot be shown to differ essentially from those trade restrictions and monopolies enacted in long series after 1688, and which the Colonies in 1765 openly recognized as legal,—in virtue of the predominance obtained at the Revolution by the commercial classes in this country.

Going, however, beyond these minor motives, the true cause was unquestionably that the time for separate life, for America to be herself, had come. This was a crisis which home-legislation could do little to create or to avert : a natural law, which only worked itself out to the eye by political manœuvres in Parliament and Congress,—and, as a 'struggle for existence,' is, on either side, in the eye of impartial history, hardly within the scope of praise or censure.

THE END

Printed by R. & R. CLARK, *Edinburgh.*

www.ingramcontent.com/pod-product-compliance
Lightning Source LLC
Chambersburg PA
CBHW020311240426
43673CB00039B/776